fun origami for children

Wild!

12 amazing animals to fold

Mari Ono & Fumiaki Shingu

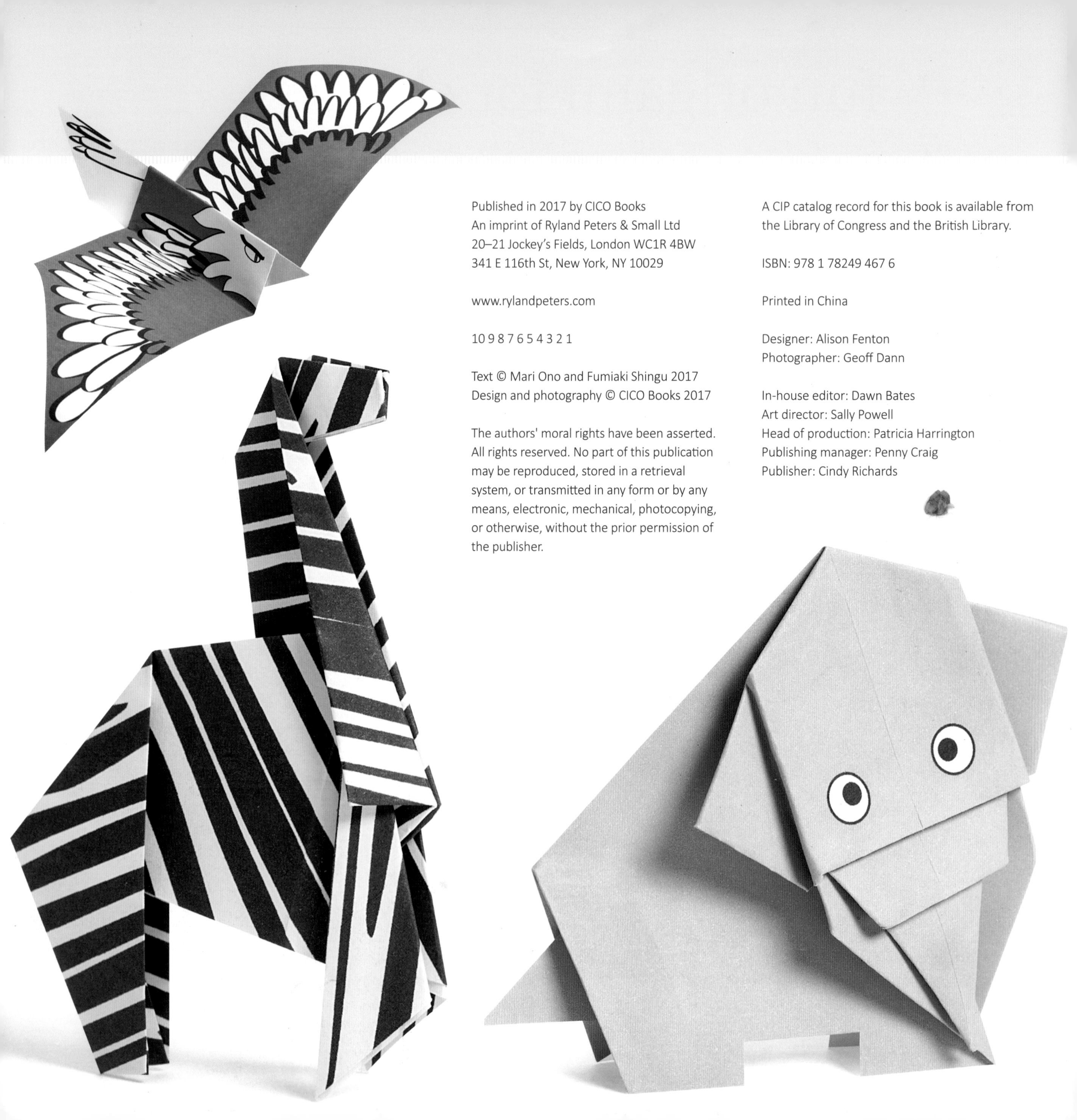

Published in 2017 by CICO Books
An imprint of Ryland Peters & Small Ltd
20–21 Jockey's Fields, London WC1R 4BW
341 E 116th St, New York, NY 10029

www.rylandpeters.com

10 9 8 7 6 5 4 3 2 1

A CIP catalog record for this book is available from the Library of Congress and the British Library.

ISBN: 978 1 78249 467 6

Printed in China

Designer: Alison Fenton
Photographer: Geoff Dann

In-house editor: Dawn Bates
Art director: Sally Powell
Head of production: Patricia Harrington
Publishing manager: Penny Craig
Publisher: Cindy Richards

Contents

Welcome to Origami!

These fun paper animals have been designed for you to make either by yourself or with a grown-up if you prefer. Begin with a simple project and learn a few basic folds before moving on to something a bit more ambitious. You'll soon find yourself picking up the skills that Japanese people have been using for centuries and making models that even origami masters would be proud of. Origami is great fun and we hope you will enjoy bringing the models to life.

Key to arrows

Fold
Fold the part of the paper shown in this direction.

Folding direction
Fold the entire paper over in this direction.

Open out
Open out and refold the paper over in the direction shown.

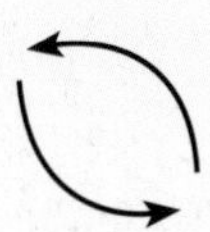

Change the position
Spin the paper 90° in the direction of the arrows.

Change the position
Spin the paper through 180°.

Turn over
Turn the paper over.

Make a crease
Fold the paper over in the direction of the arrow, then open it out again.

Look for the penguins!

A good project to start with

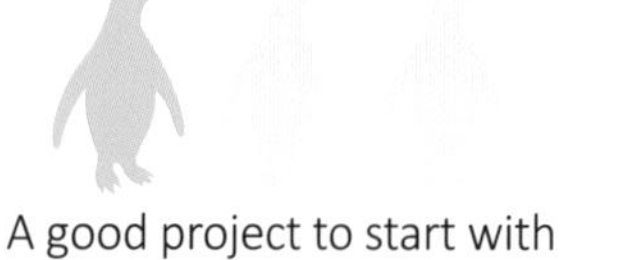

Move on to level 2

Perfect your skills with level 3

Basic Techniques

Origami is a very simple craft that simply requires a steady hand and some patience. Before you start making your first model, just check over these simple tips to ensure every paper model you make is a success.

Making folds Making the paper fold as crisply and evenly as possible is the key to making models that will stand up as the designs intend—it really is as simple as that.

1 When you make a fold ensure that the paper lies exactly where you want it, with the corners sitting exactly on top of each other.

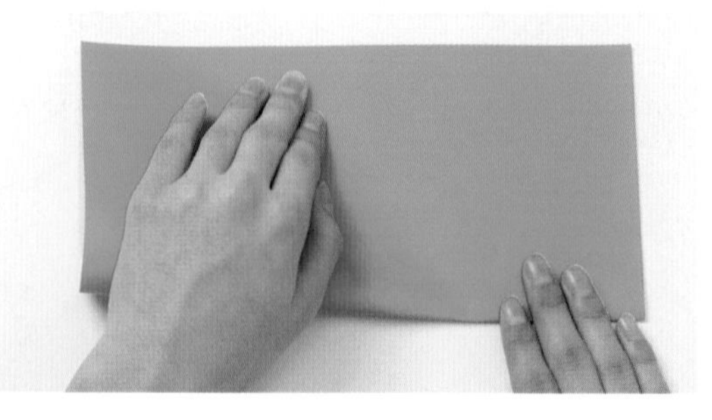

2 As you make the crease, be sure to keep the paper completely still so that the fold is straight.

3 Use a ruler or perhaps the side of a pencil to press down the fold until it is as flat as possible.

Opening folds Sometimes you will need to open out a crease and refold the paper so that it lies in a new shape, as in the triangle fold shown here.

1 Lift the flap to be opened out and begin pulling the two sides apart.

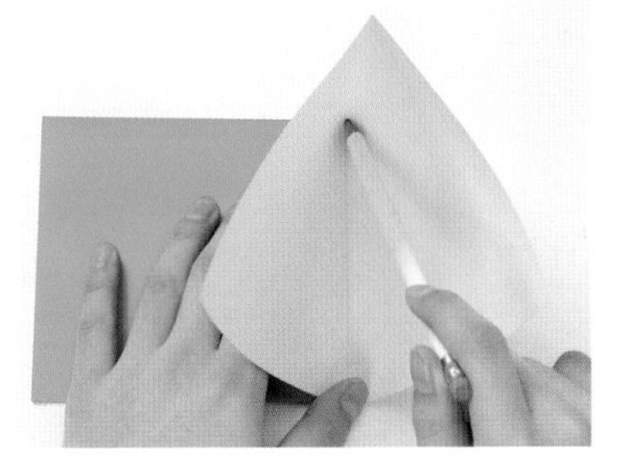

2 As the space widens you will need to be sure that the far point folds correctly, so use a pencil to gently prise the paper open.

3 As the two corners separate, the top point drops forward and the two edges open out to become one.

4 Press down the new creases to make the two new angled sides of the triangle.

Reversing folds To reverse a crease you will need to open out your model and gently turn part of the paper back on itself. This can be tricky so practice on a spare piece of paper first.

1 To turn the tip back on itself, first make a firm crease with a simple fold.

2 Return the tip back to its original position and open out the model. Turn back the nose again along the fold you just made.

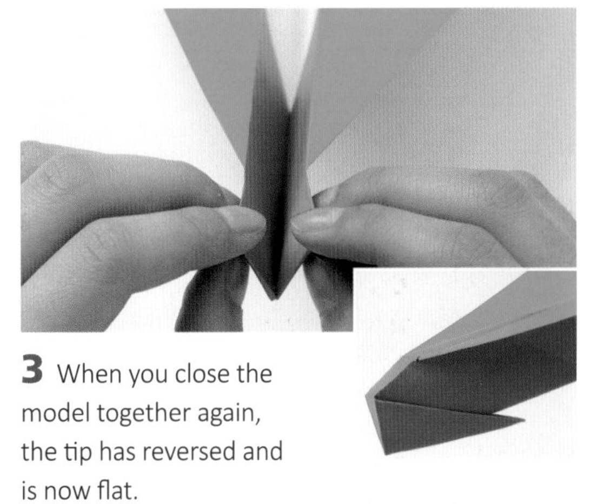

3 When you close the model together again, the tip has reversed and is now flat.

When you're using scissors, ask a grown-up to supervise or help.

Ed the Eagle

The sky is ruled by the birds and the most magnificent of them all—the king—is the eagle. You could hang this magnificent one from your bedroom ceiling.

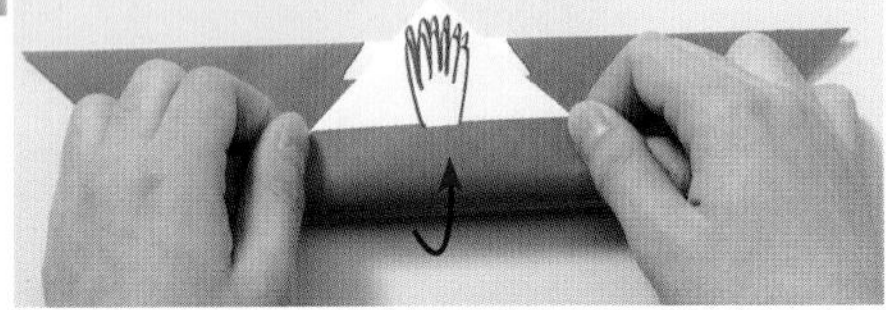

1 Fold the sheet of 10in (25cm) paper in half to make a crease from corner to corner along the length of the design, then open it out and make another fold between the side corners. Turn back both tips from the bottom so that they cross the horizontal fold by about 1in (2.5cm), checking that the edges align along the white diagonals in the design.

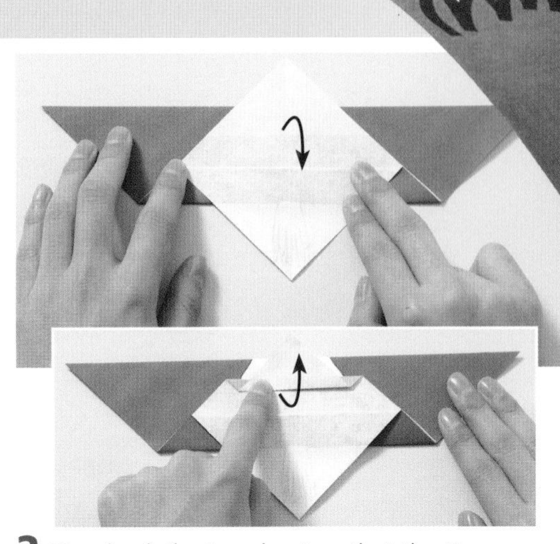

2 Turn back the top sheet so that the tip crosses the model's bottom edge by about 1in (2.5cm), checking that the design showing through the paper aligns with the bottom of the model. Fold back the other tip on the far side of the model along the edge of the design, then turn the flap back about ½in (1cm) from the new tip.

3 Fold the model in half to reinforce the central crease, then turn the top flap to the right to make a wing, aligning the new crease along the top of the model's head.

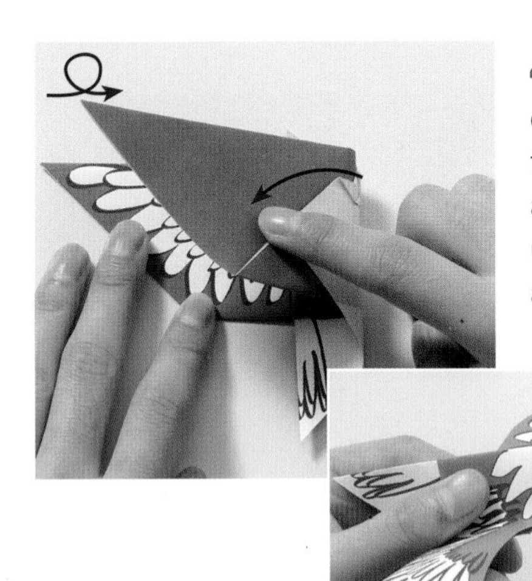

4 Turn the paper over, then fold over the other wing to match the first. To finish, open out the model and run your finger along the underside of the wings to give them a curve to resemble flight.

Gotcha! An eagle's powerful talons help it to catch its prey.

Saira the Snake

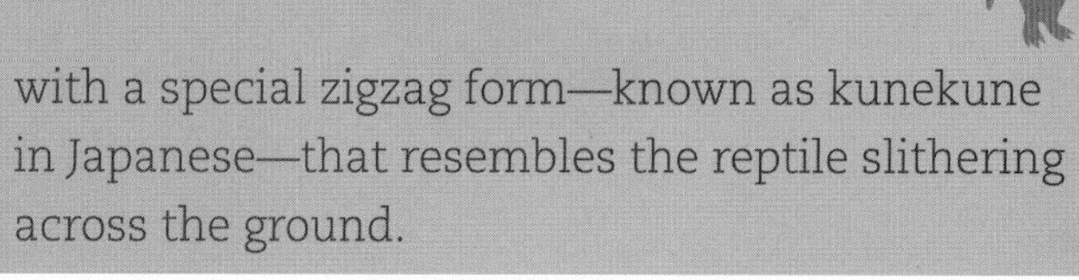

It may surprise you that there are over 3,000 different kinds of snakes and this book will show you how to make one of them—but only if you are brave enough! The design is made with a special zigzag form—known as kunekune in Japanese—that resembles the reptile slithering across the ground.

1 Fold the sheet of 10in (25cm) paper in half from corner to corner to make a crease between the eyes. Open out again and fold in the two right-hand edges so that they meet on the central crease, then repeat so that the two creased edges meet.

2 Now fold in the two short edges on the left-hand end of the paper so that they also meet in the center, then fold the model in half.

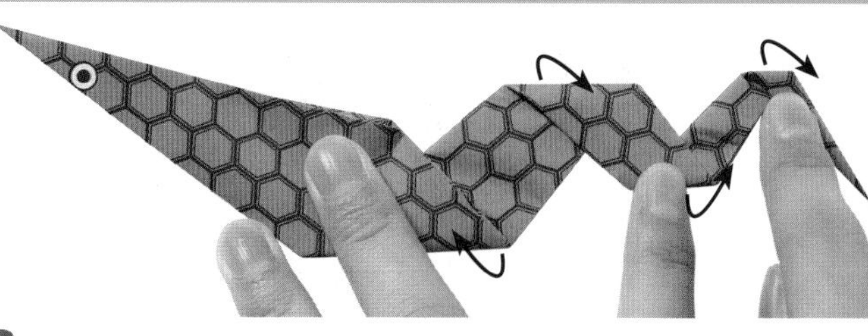

3 Keeping the head still, fold the body underneath at an angle, starting about 6in (15cm) from the left-hand tip. Next, fold the body over again three more times in the same direction, ensuring that the sections are all a similar length. Now open up the model and reverse each set of creases in turn, starting at the head. When each one is complete hold it in place as you move along the model.

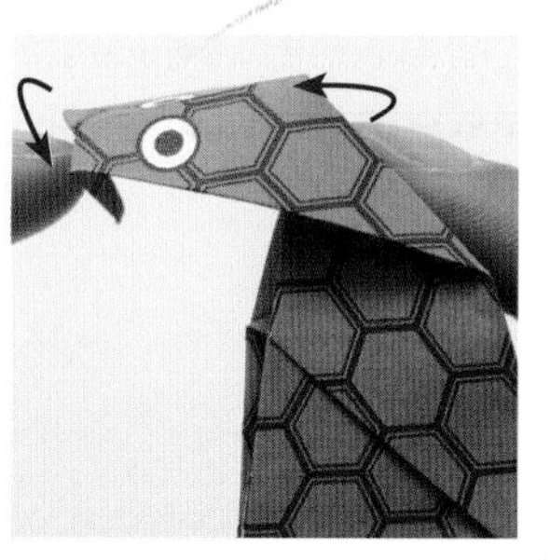

4 To finish, make a pair of creases across the head about 3in (7cm) from the tip of the nose, reverse them, and then fold up the tip inside to give the model a flat nose.

Gulp! Snakes can't bite or chew food—instead they swallow it whole!

Gee Gee the Giraffe

No safari scene would be complete without the appearance of the beautiful and graceful giraffe, the tallest creature in the animal kingdom. Their height keeps them safe, as they are able to spot predators from a long way off. Giraffes are social animals that travel in groups, so we've given you an extra sheet of paper to make a friend for Gee Gee!

1 Fold the sheet of 10in (25cm) paper in half from corner to corner and open out, then fold in the two upper edges so that they meet along the central crease. Fold the paper in half along the crease.

2 Fold the top point down and across to the left, making a diagonal crease up and across the paper from just above the right-hand point.

3 Open out the paper and reverse the creases made in the previous step, refolding the paper so that the flap now surrounds the main body of the model.

4 Fold over the tip of the flap and make a crease, then open the flap out, reverse the creases just made, and refold so that the tip surrounds the rest of the flap.

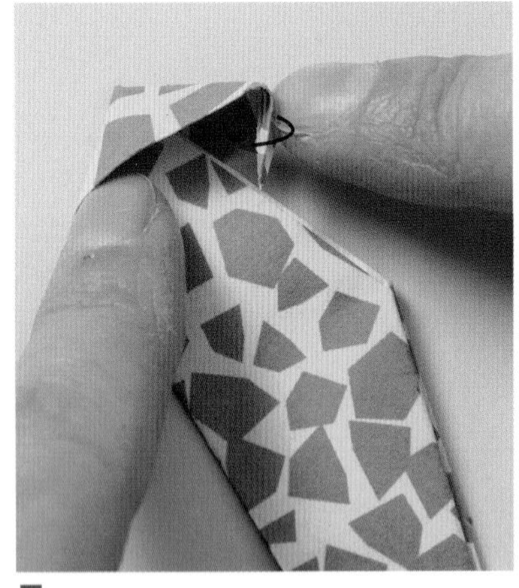

5 Fold the tip over again about ½in (1cm) from the end and reverse the creases, so that the tip can be folded inside.

6 Turn over the bottom left corner at a slight angle by about 2in (5cm) and make a crease to begin making the giraffe's tail. Turn over the tip a second time so that the corner points up slightly and sticks out from the model.

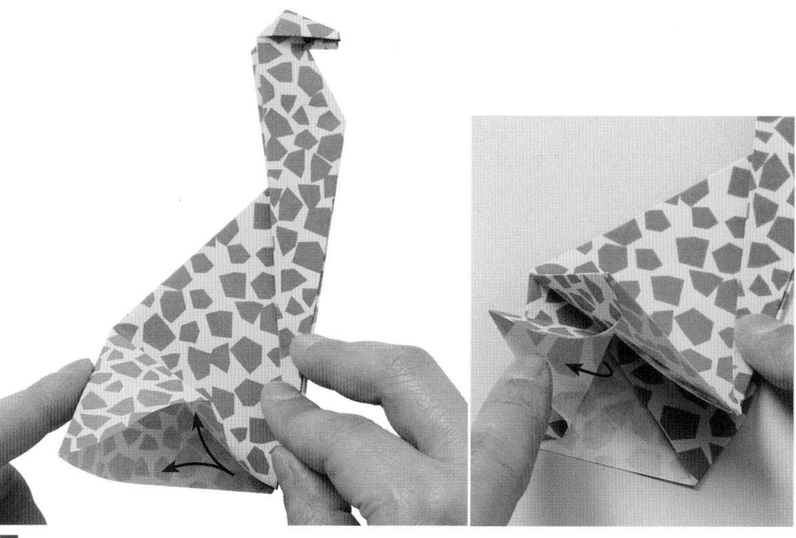

7 Open out the bottom of the model and fold in the tail, reversing the first crease made in the previous step, then reverse the second crease so that the tail sticks out from inside the model.

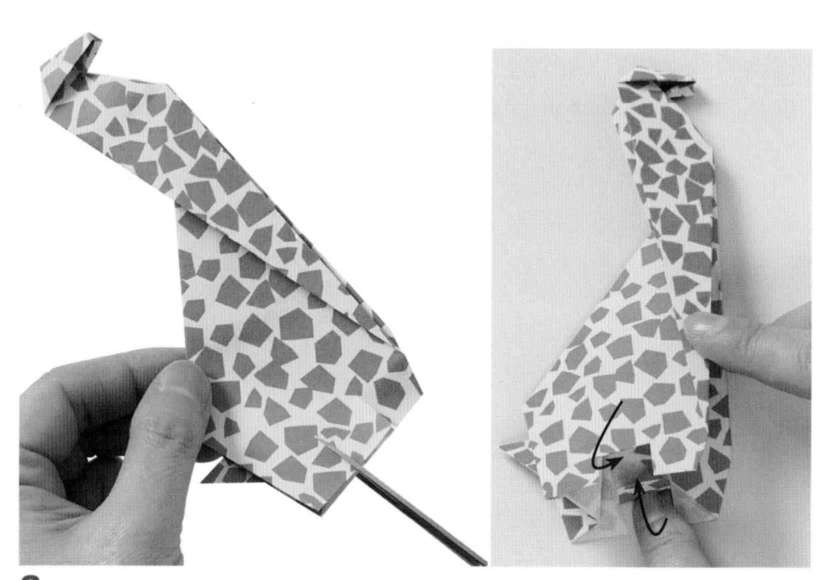

8 Cut twice through the bottom edges of the model and fold up the loose paper to reveal the giraffe's legs.

Greedy?! A giraffe can consume up to 100lb (45kg) of twigs in a day!

Caz the Chameleon

Brighten up your origami collection with this colorful chameleon. It is one of the most weird and wonderful creatures on earth, able to change its skin color to suit its environment. Watch it change from green to yellow to blue at will, always hiding from its enemies. Its presence hidden, the chameleon quietly waits to catch insects for food.

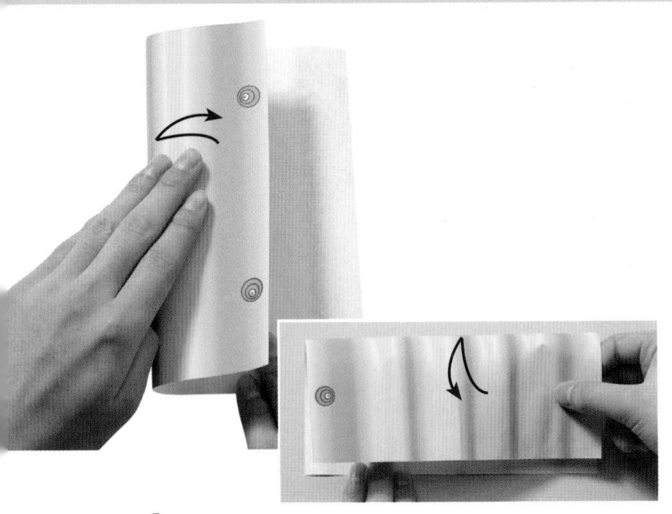

1 Place the sheet of 10in (25cm) paper with the design face down and the eyes on the left, fold the paper in half from left to right, make a crease, and open it out again. Repeat the fold from top to bottom, again opening the sheet out afterward.

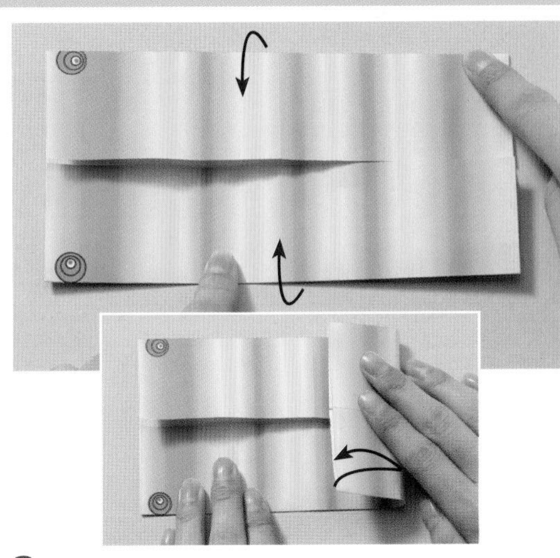

2 Fold the top and bottom edges so that they meet along the horizontal crease, then fold in both ends so that they also meet in the middle, make creases, then open them out.

3 Make a pair of triangle folds at each end by lifting one side of the top flap of paper at a time, folding the corner across the crease made in the previous step to the middle of the model, and refolding it to form a triangle.

4 Turn the paper over and fold in the four diagonal edges, starting at the right-hand side, so that the two at each end meet along the central crease.

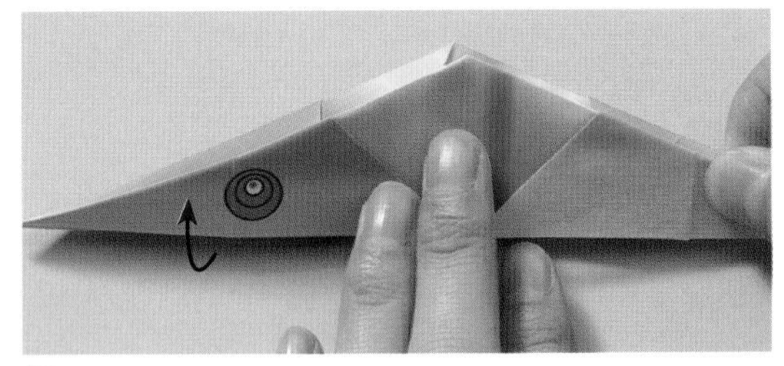

5 Fold the bottom of the model over, reversing the central crease.

6 Fold over the two loose triangles on each side of the model to form the chameleon's legs. Ensure that one side of the triangle is vertical even though this means the tips of the triangles will fall below the main edge of the model.

Moody! The chameleon changes to a dark color when it's angry!

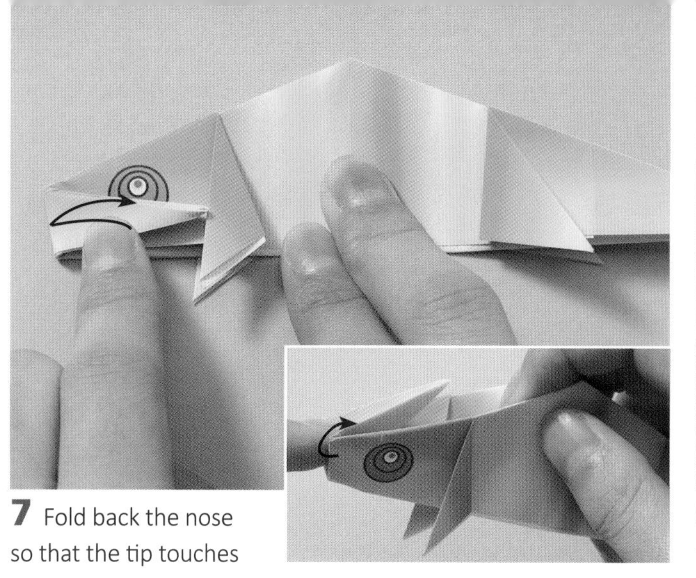

7 Fold back the nose so that the tip touches the model's front leg and make a vertical crease, then open out the body and fold the tip back inside, reversing the creases.

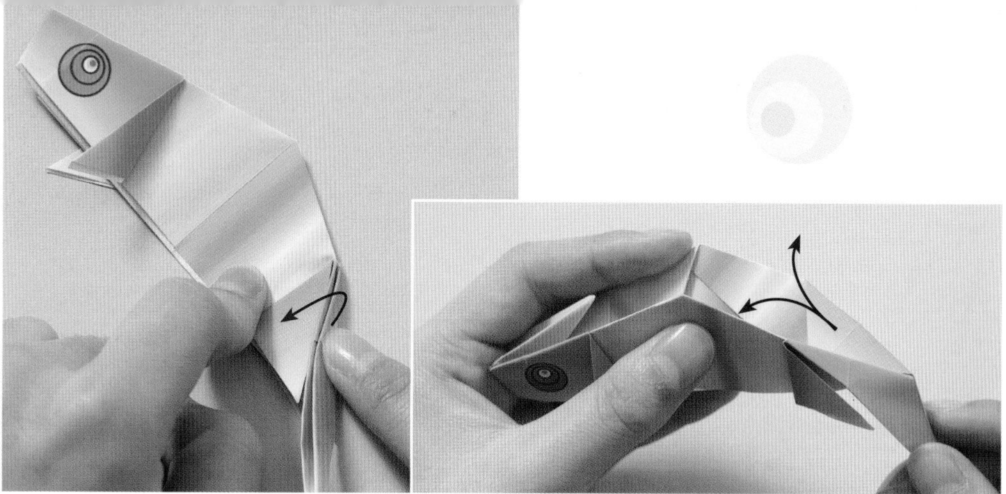

8 Fold forward the tail of the model at an angle, then open out the body and reverse the creases so that the tail surrounds the body of the model.

9 Make another fold in the tail and open it out to reverse the creases so that the tip is surrounded by the bulk of the tail.

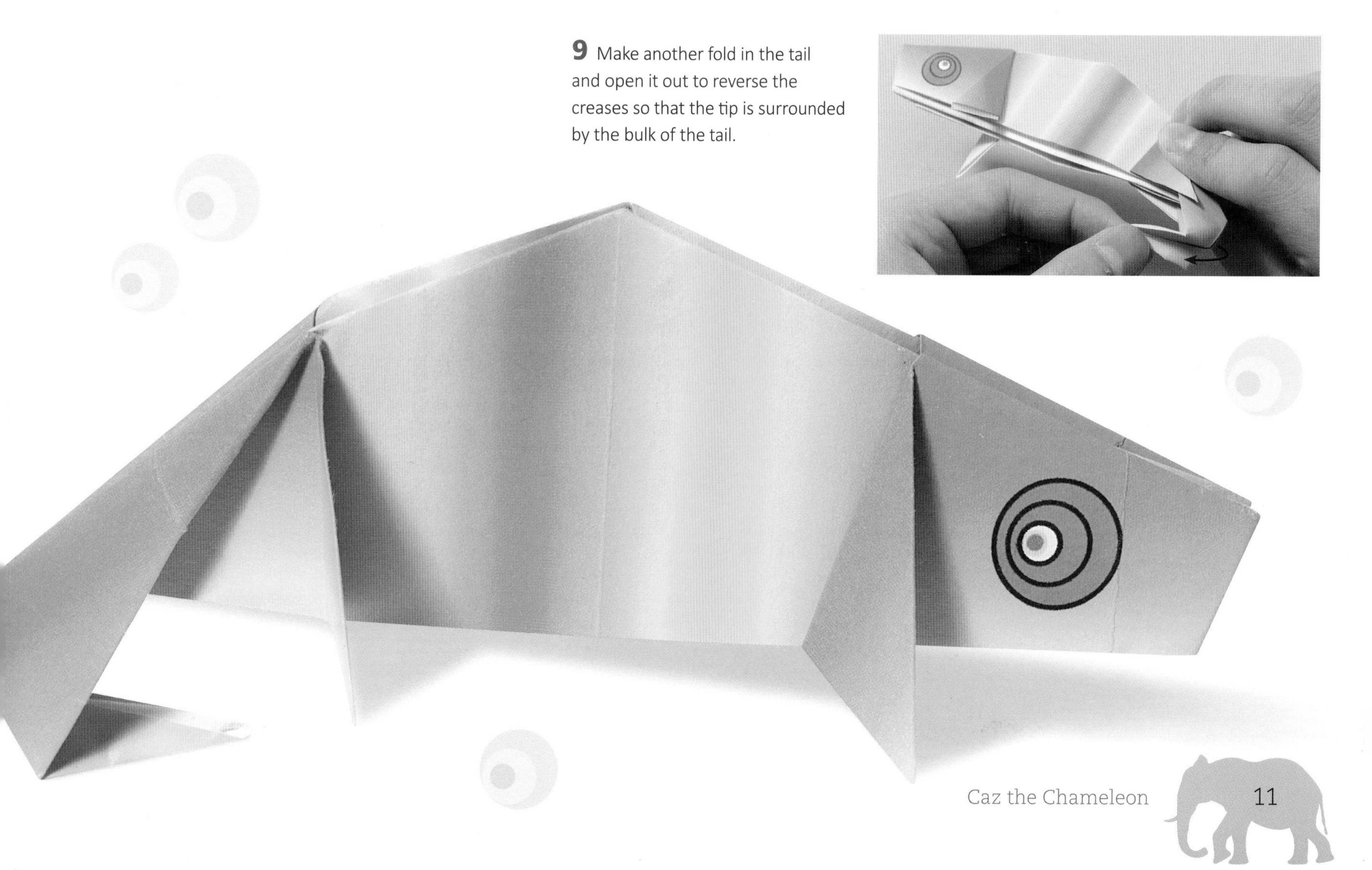

Zak the Zebra

The herds of zebras that run majestically across the African savannah are one of the greatest sights of a safari. Their distinctive black and white markings are key to their survival—as they run as a herd, their stripes merge and it is difficult for predators to make out individuals to attack. Keep your stripy friend, Zak, standing up because that's how zebras sleep!

1 Fold the sheet of 10in (25cm) paper from corner to corner across the design and open out. Next fold over the two sides on the left so that their edges meet along the central crease, and repeat on the right.

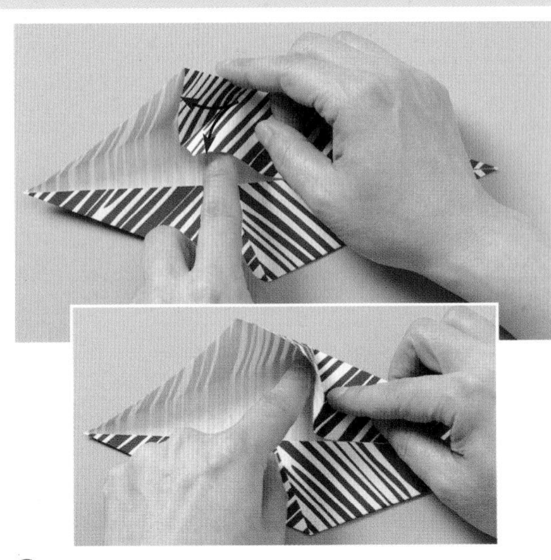

2 Lift the top flap on the left and begin to reverse the inside crease, pushing up the corner of the paper to open out all the folds.

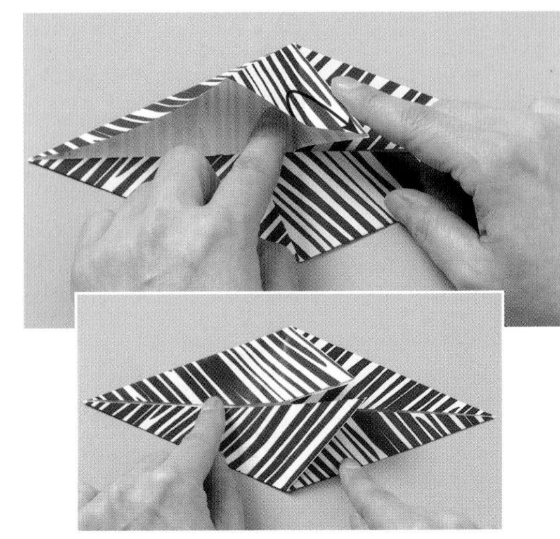

3 Push the corner of the paper to the right so that it sits on the central crease and press down so that the edge of the paper also runs along the central fold. Repeat on the bottom half of the model.

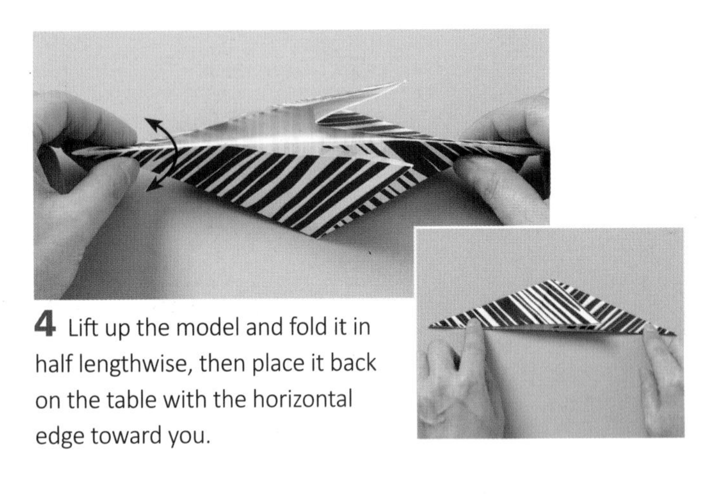

4 Lift up the model and fold it in half lengthwise, then place it back on the table with the horizontal edge toward you.

5 Turn the left-hand point so that the bottom edge runs vertically through the model's midpoint and make a crease to form the neck, then open out the model and fold the neck inside, reversing all the creases.

Unique! A zebra has an individual pattern, just like a human fingerprint!

6 Turn over the top of the neck to form the head. Open out the neck and fold the head inside, reversing the direction of the creases.

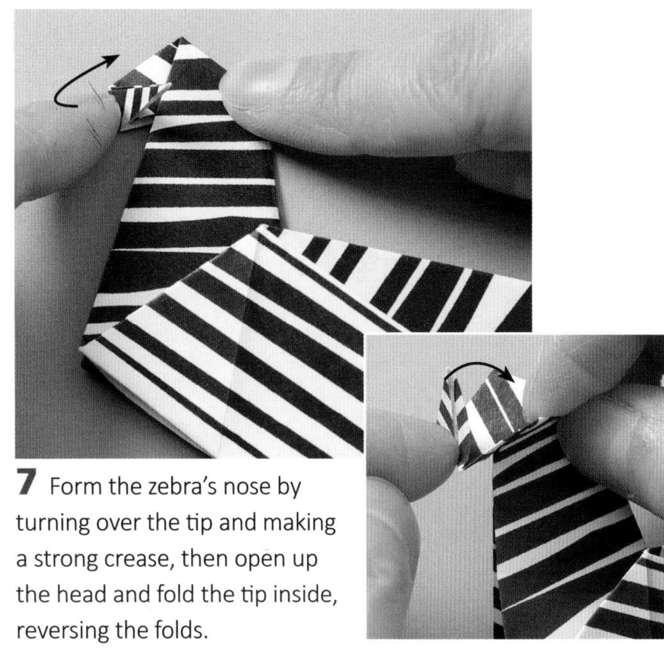

7 Form the zebra's nose by turning over the tip and making a strong crease, then open up the head and fold the tip inside, reversing the folds.

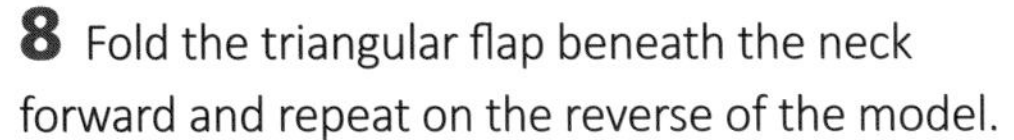

8 Fold the triangular flap beneath the neck forward and repeat on the reverse of the model.

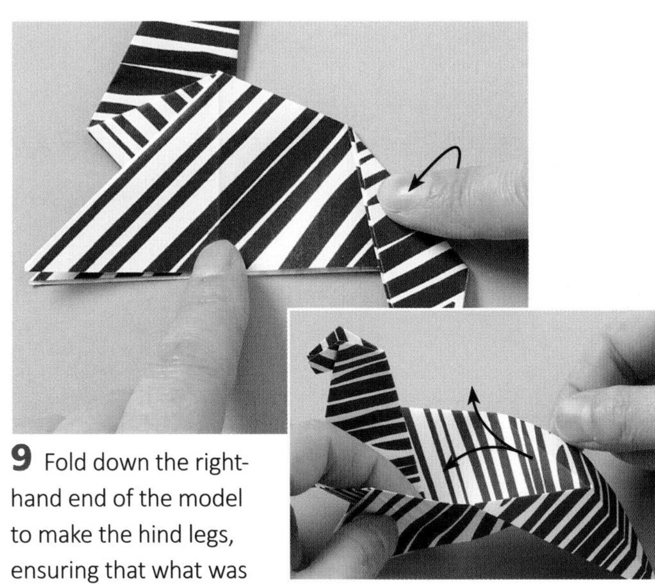

9 Fold down the right-hand end of the model to make the hind legs, ensuring that what was the top edge now runs down at a slight angle. Open out the body of the zebra and reverse the creases, folding the legs around the outside of the body.

10 Fold over the top left-hand triangle to form one of the front legs, again ensuring that the top edge now runs straight down. Repeat on the reverse.

11 Fold back the front edge of the neck, making a vertical crease from the highest point of the head. Lift up the zebra and repeat on the back.

12 To finish, fold up the bottom of the hind legs and make a crease, then open out the legs and tuck the tip up inside, reversing the creases.

Max the Monkey

Monkeys are particularly well-known for the amusing looks they give their companions as their large families scramble through the trees. We think this one has real character!

Choose one of the various positions for its arm—either bent so that he can hang from a branch, in a folded position, or ready to eat a banana.

1 Fold the 10in (25cm) sheet of paper in half from corner to corner through the middle of the design, then fold it in half again.

2 Lift the top flap, opening it out and refolding so the point sits on top of the bottom of the paper. Turn the paper over and repeat so that the model is shaped like a diamond.

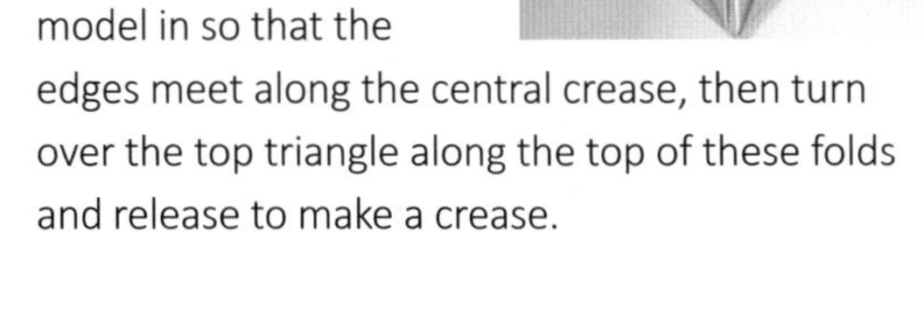

3 Fold the upper flap on each side of the model in so that the edges meet along the central crease, then turn over the top triangle along the top of these folds and release to make a crease.

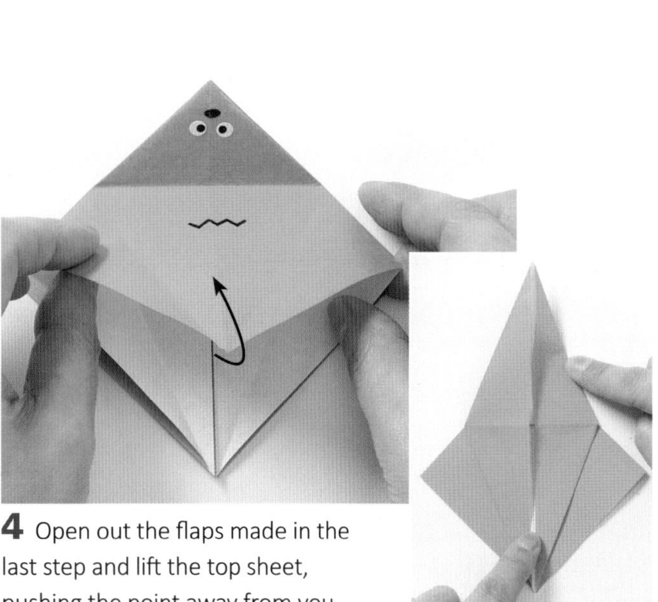

4 Open out the flaps made in the last step and lift the top sheet, pushing the point away from you. Refold so that a long diamond is formed.

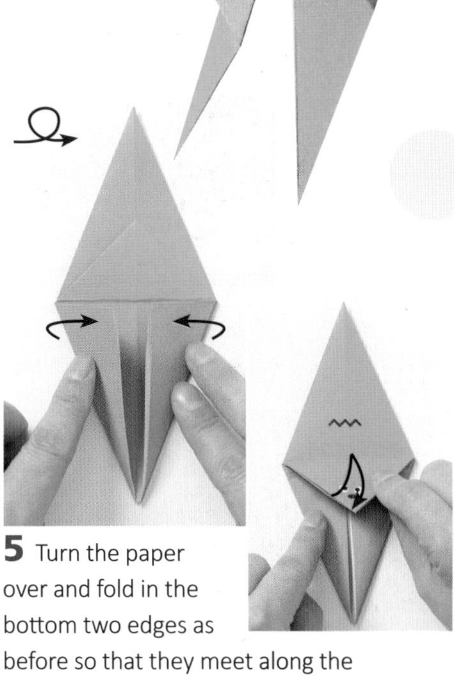

5 Turn the paper over and fold in the bottom two edges as before so that they meet along the central crease, then fold forward the triangle in the middle of the model to make a crease and release.

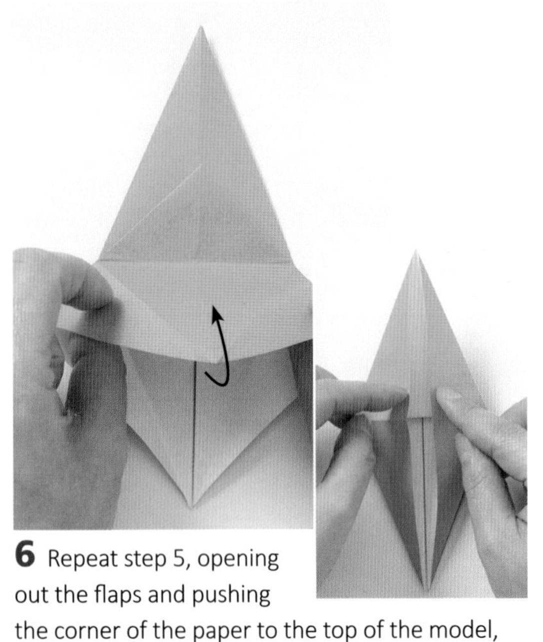

6 Repeat step 5, opening out the flaps and pushing the corner of the paper to the top of the model, flattening the sides to make a thin diamond shape.

7 Fold in the top flaps on each side so that the lower edges meet along the model's central crease.

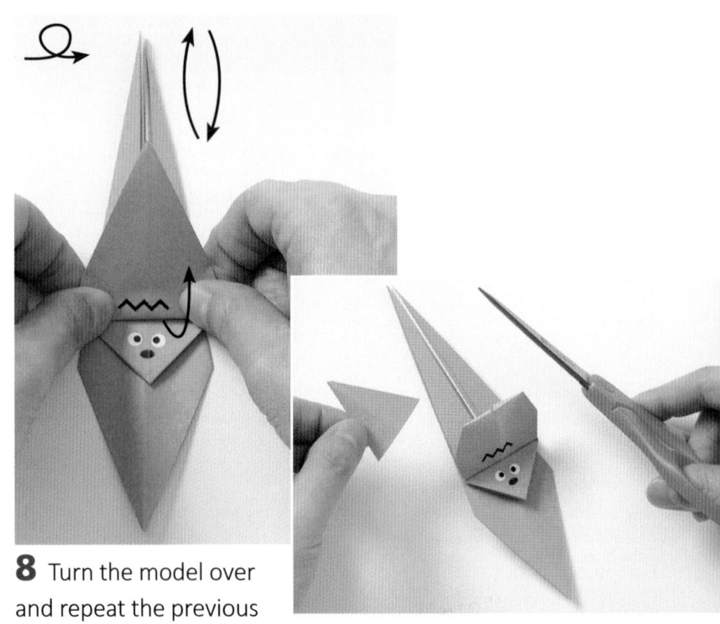

8 Turn the model over and repeat the previous step, folding the edges into the center to match, then spin the paper through 180° and lift the flap nearest you to the vertical and make a crease. Next cut off the top of the flap with the scissors about 2in (5cm) from the crease.

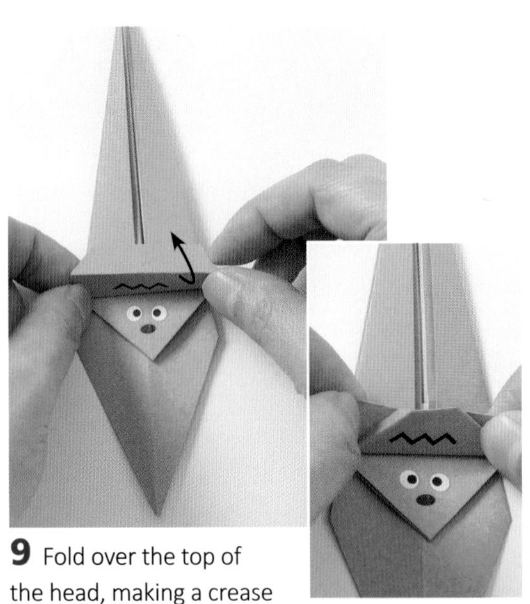

9 Fold over the top of the head, making a crease about ¾in (2cm) from the end, then fold back the corners before making a second crease and folding them out again to make the ears.

10 Turn over the right-hand arm and make a crease then open out the arm and reverse the creases, folding the end inside.

11 Repeat further down the arm to make the elbow, making the crease about halfway along the arm so that the end crosses over the body when folded.

12 Repeat the two creases and reverse folds on the other arm, making both creases much closer to end to indicate a hanging arm.

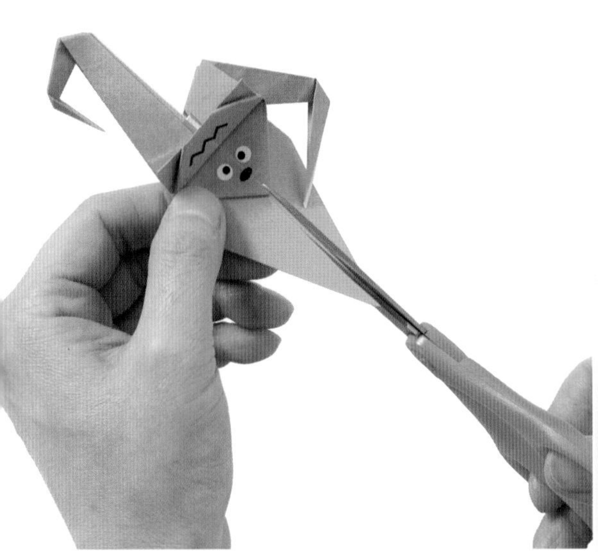

13 Use the scissors to cut up the body, then fold the ends underneath at a slight angle to make the legs.

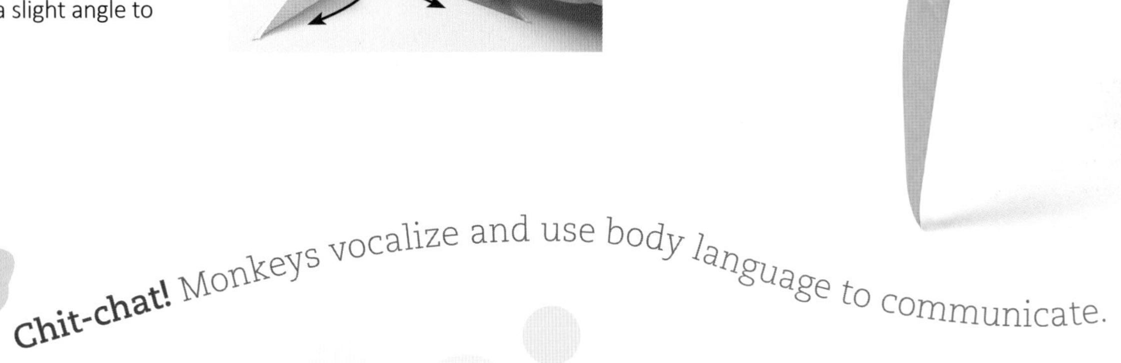

Chit-chat! Monkeys vocalize and use body language to communicate.

Lotto the Lion

Enjoy making your very own king of the jungle. The lion is the animal most closely associated with the African plains. Seeing these magnificent creatures stalk through the undergrowth before bringing down their prey is a scene that can only be witnessed on safari. The face on this model shows the lion's glare, as he gets ready to pounce!

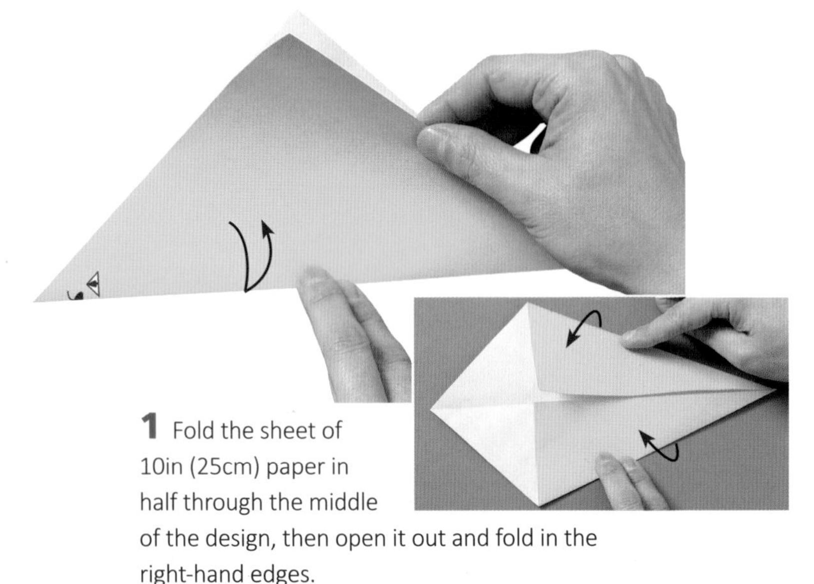

1 Fold the sheet of 10in (25cm) paper in half through the middle of the design, then open it out and fold in the right-hand edges.

2 Fold each flap's short edge underneath itself, making a crease from the top and bottom corners to a point about 2in (5cm) down the long edge so that they both meet along the central crease.

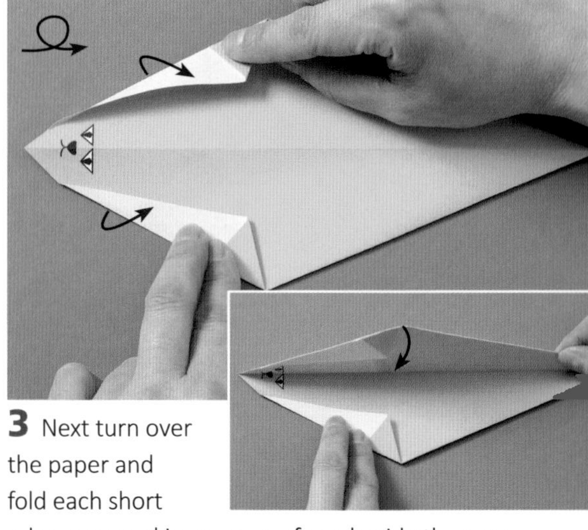

3 Next turn over the paper and fold each short edge over, making a crease from beside the nose to a point 2in (5cm) beyond the top and bottom corners, then fold the paper in half.

4 Fold over the left-hand tip, making a diagonal crease from a point two-thirds of the way along the lower edge so that the tip folds down and toward the right.

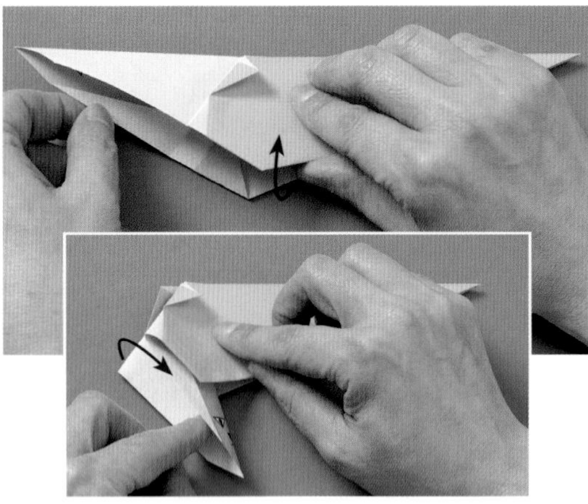

5 Lift the top flap from the bottom and bring the left-hand point across and down, folding it inside the model so that the creases are reversed.

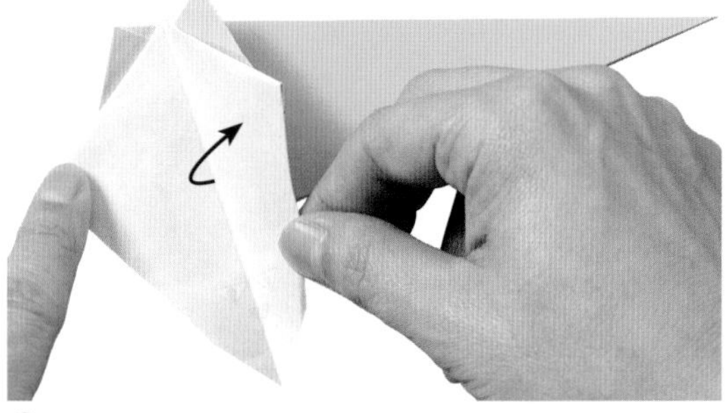

6 Lift the top flap on the model's left-hand side and fold it to the right to make a diamond shape.

So lazy! Male lions leave 85–90% of the hunting to the lionesses!

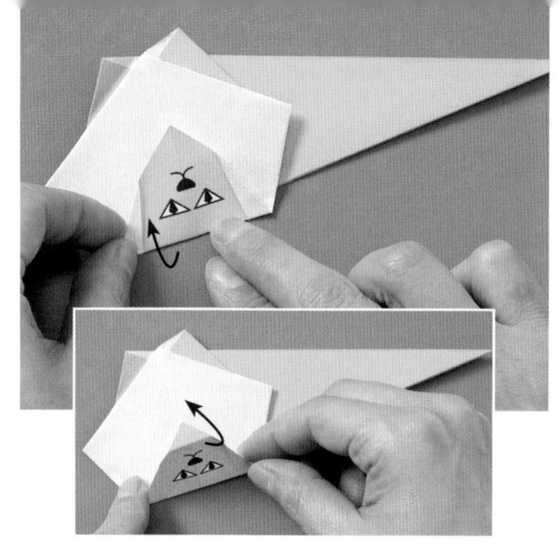

7 Turn over the bend of this diamond to form the lion's face, making a crease about ½in (1cm) out from the model's main edge and in line with it. Then turn over the tip of the face to form a flat chin.

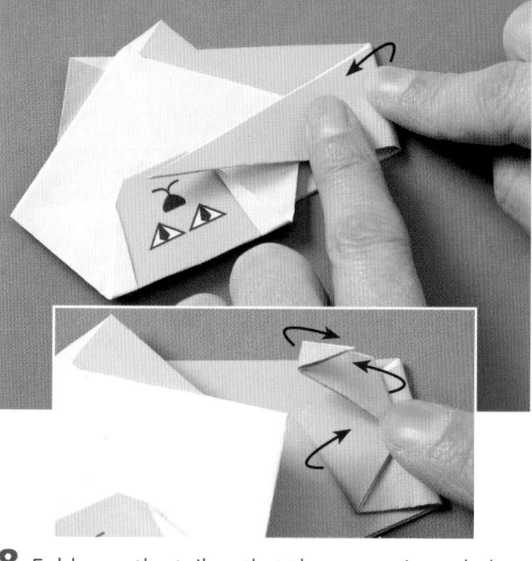

8 Fold over the tail so that the crease is angled slightly upward, then make three more folds along its length to form the curls of the tail.

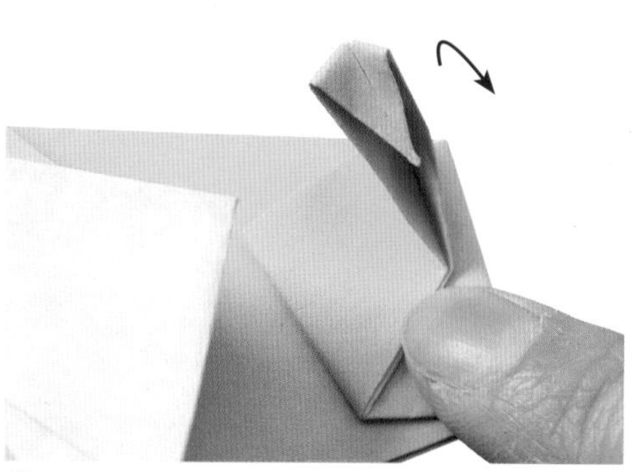

9 Open out the last fold in the tail and turn the end inside, reversing the creases so that it sits flat.

10 Turn the flap below the head across the main edge of the model and make a crease. This edge should sit away from the back of the model and act as a stand for the model.

Gus the Gorilla

The gorilla is one of the rarest species on Earth as well as one of the most popular in the zoo. But what do they do during their days in the wild? When not eating the grass, fruits, and insects, they are walking on their knuckles. This origami model—showing the gorilla in this pose—is a traditional design from Japan.

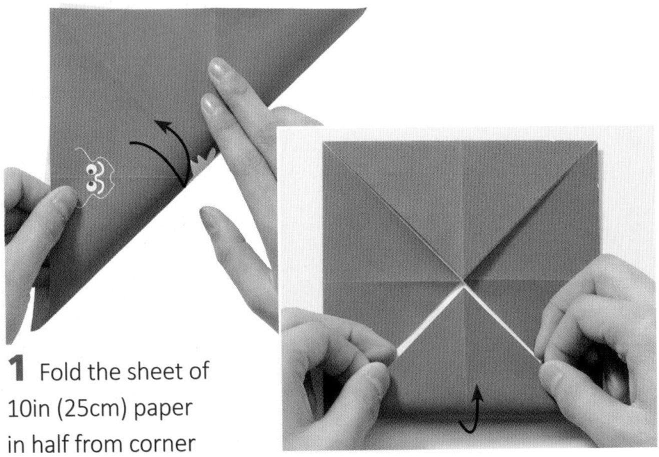

1 Fold the sheet of 10in (25cm) paper in half from corner to corner, then open it out and repeat in the other direction. Open out again and fold in half both ways across the sheet, then fold all four corners in so that they meet at the center point.

2 Turn the paper through 45° and fold in the top and bottom corners, ensuring that one of them includes the design for the gorilla's face.

3 Turn the paper over and fold the bottom right-hand corner up to the center point, ensuring that the bottom right edge now runs vertically along the model's central crease line. Repeat on the left-hand side.

4 Make angled creases on the upper flaps from the model's outer points to the center and fold the flaps over.

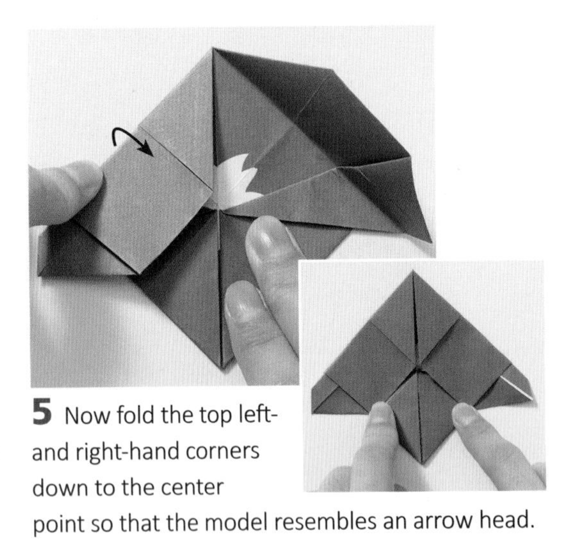

5 Now fold the top left- and right-hand corners down to the center point so that the model resembles an arrow head.

6 Lift the upper right-hand flap and reverse the inner crease, before flattening the flap and folding the reversed sheet around the outside. Repeat on the left-hand side.

Boohoo... Gorillas are known to express grief as well as compassion.

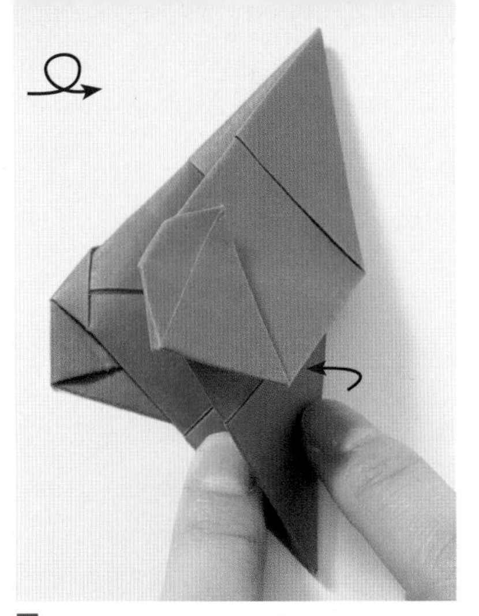

7 Turn the model over and carefully fold it in half along the central vertical crease.

8 Make the model's feet by opening up the flap in the middle of the model and folding the long edge over. The feet and legs will not fold flat—let them splay open.

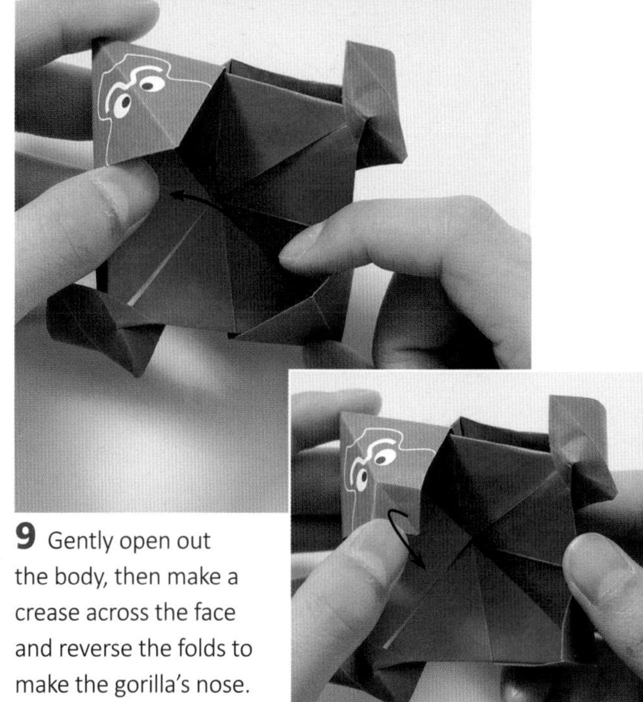

9 Gently open out the body, then make a crease across the face and reverse the folds to make the gorilla's nose.

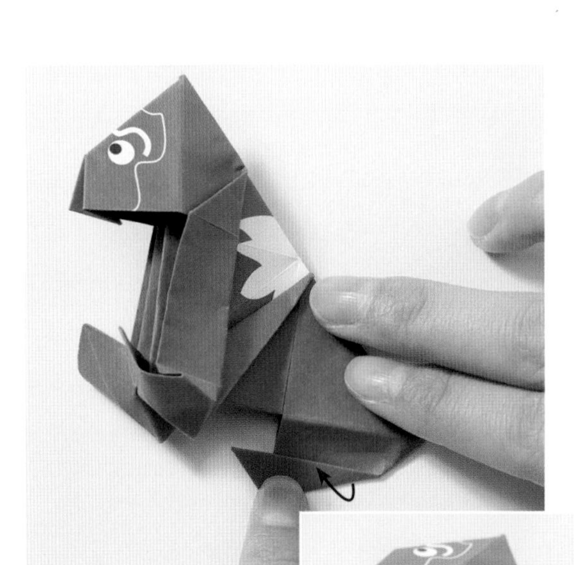

10 Fold up the bottom 1in (2.5cm) of the model to make a stand for the gorilla.

Charlie the Cheetah

This origami model may look like a little like a sweet pussy cat, but the cheetah is strong and wild and, as the fastest animal on Earth, no other creatures on the African plain can keep up with it! Did you know that the cheetah's tail is essential to its speed? They use it to steer and balance themselves as they run.

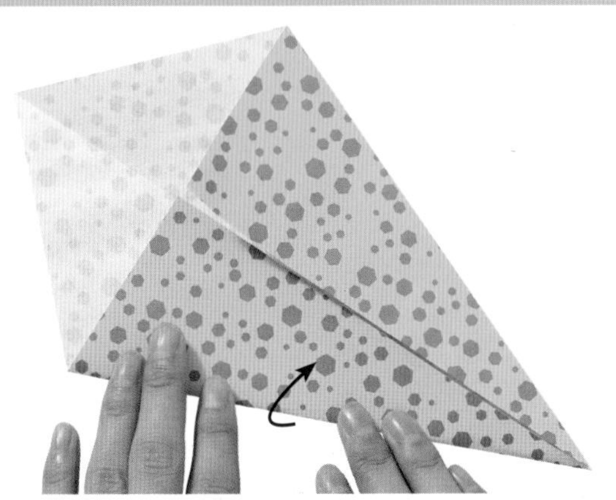

1 Fold the sheet of 10in (25cm) paper in half from corner to corner through the design of the face, then fold in the edges at the face so that they meet along the central crease.

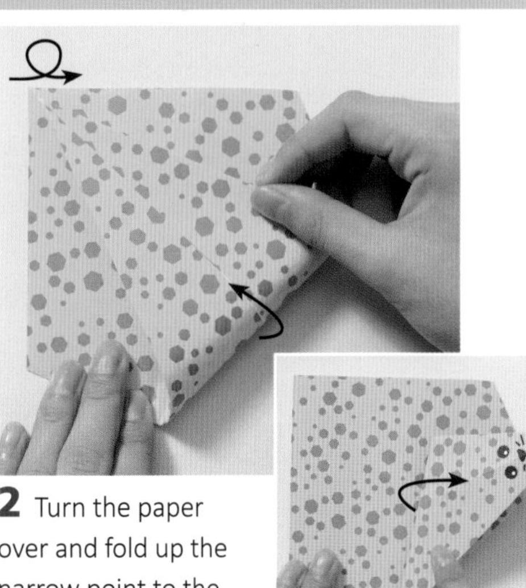

2 Turn the paper over and fold up the narrow point to the opposite corner and make a crease, then fold the narrow point down to the right so that the left-hand edge now runs along the bottom of the model.

3 Pick up the paper and fold the left-hand side of the model underneath along the central crease, then fold the narrow point to the left so that its top long edge turns over and sits on top of the other edge. Fold what is now the upper edge of the long point over from the model's bottom right-hand corner and make a crease so that the tip stands up vertically.

4 Bend the head forward so that it aligns with the crease down the model's neck and turn the nose underneath to form a flat chin. Next turn back the top corners before turning them back on themselves again to form the ears.

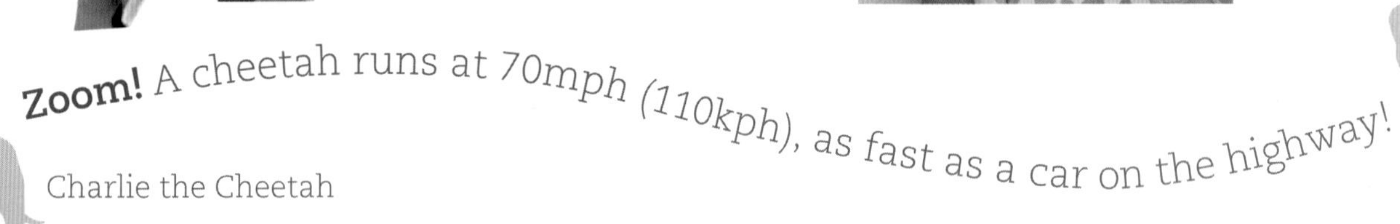

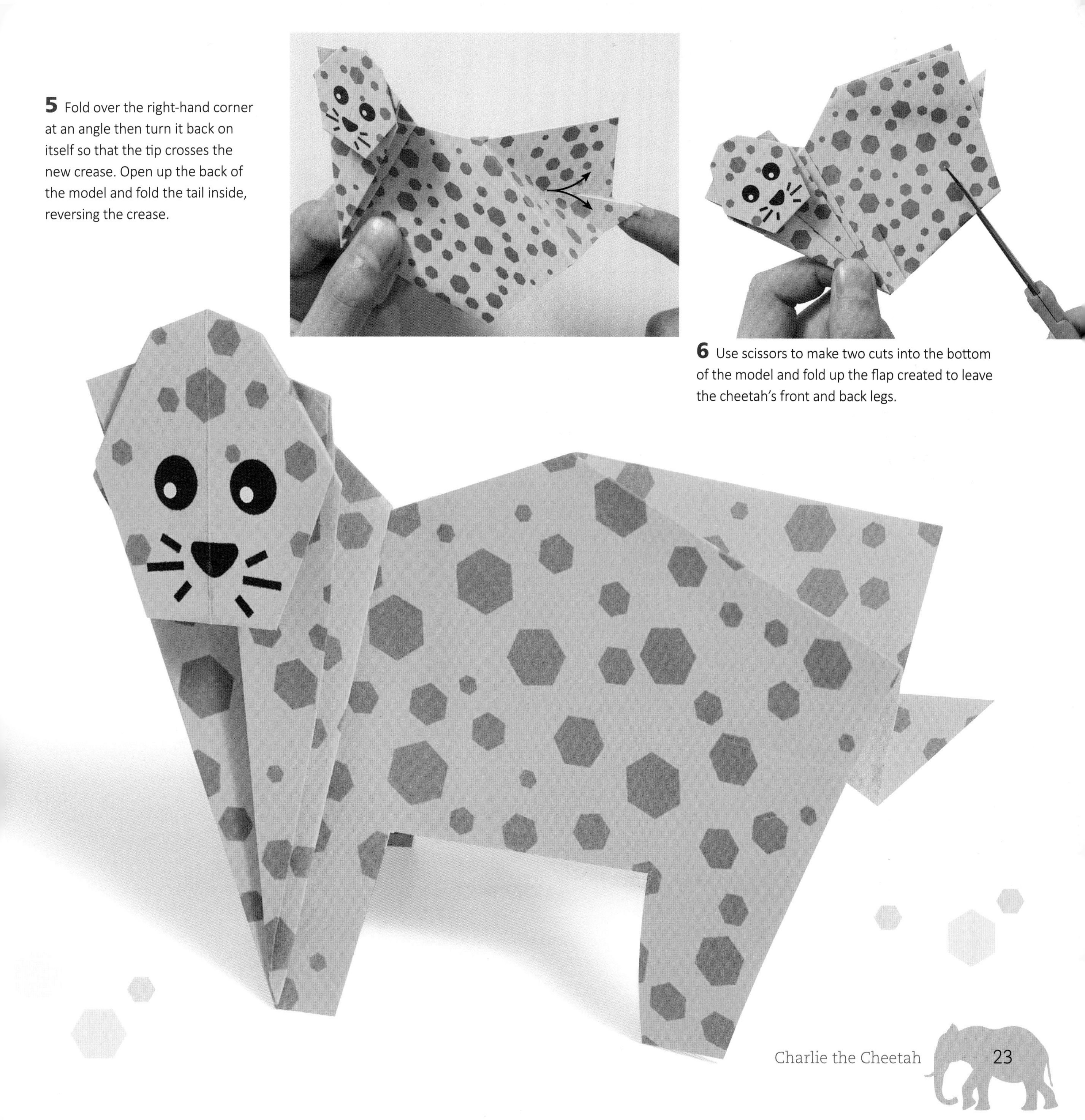

5 Fold over the right-hand corner at an angle then turn it back on itself so that the tip crosses the new crease. Open up the back of the model and fold the tail inside, reversing the crease.

6 Use scissors to make two cuts into the bottom of the model and fold up the flap created to leave the cheetah's front and back legs.

Patsy the Panda

Pandas live in the thick bamboo forests of central China. They are believed to have lived on Earth for the past 2–3 million years, but are sadly now almost extinct, with only around 1,000 living in the wild. These adorable bears are recognizable by their distinctive black and white markings. We hope you enjoy making your very own Patsy the Panda to share your home.

1 Use scissors or a scalpel and metal ruler to divide the 10in (25cm) sheet of paper into thirds, leaving two thirds for the body and one third for the head of the panda.

2 Start making the head with the paper face down. Fold it in half to make a crease then open it out again and fold the sides down and forward at an angle so that the top edges now align along the central crease. Now turn up the bottom edges, making horizontal creases from the angled corners, even though these will not necessarily exactly match the edge of the design.

3 Turn over the model and pull open the right-hand flap from underneath, then fold it up at an angle so that the bottom edge of the triangle now runs up the center of the model with the rectangular flap to the side. Now repeat on the left-hand side of the model.

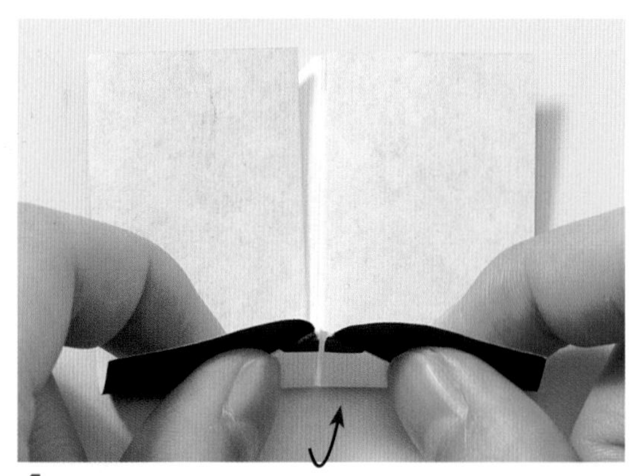

4 Fold up the bottom of the model, making a new crease about 1in (2.5cm) up the paper.

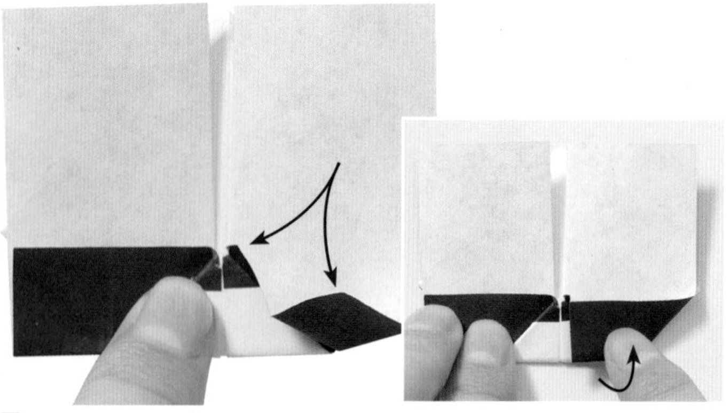

5 With your left forefinger holding down the central triangle lift the right-hand flap and open it out, refolding it so that the corner now sits on the tip of the triangle and a new crease has been made along the bottom of the model. Repeat on the other side.

6 Turning the paper over, lift it up and tuck the top corners behind to make the ears, then turn the paper over again and fold back the triangle at the top of the head. This makes the ears angled.

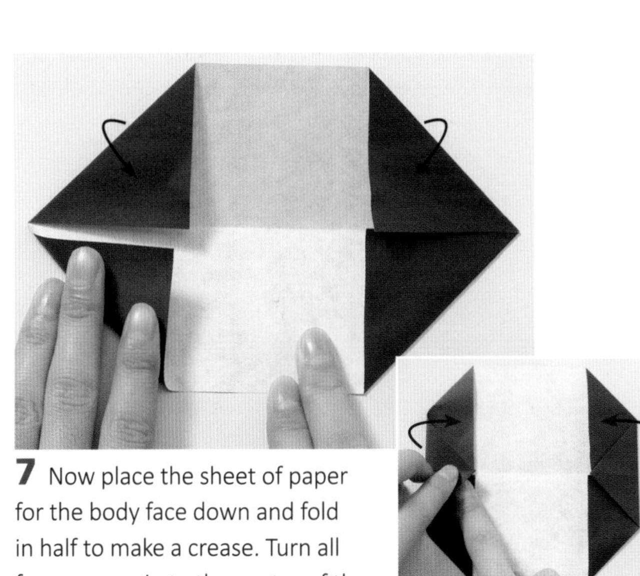

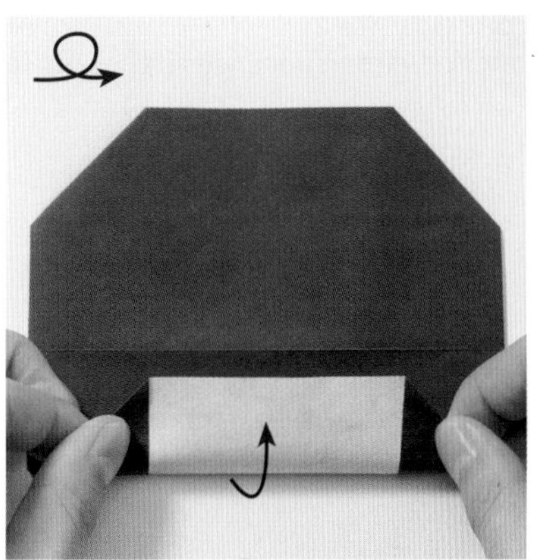

7 Now place the sheet of paper for the body face down and fold in half to make a crease. Turn all four corners in to the center of the model, then fold over the tips at either end, ensuring they end up sitting on top of the folded corners.

8 Turn the paper over and fold the bottom and top edges over so they meet along the center crease.

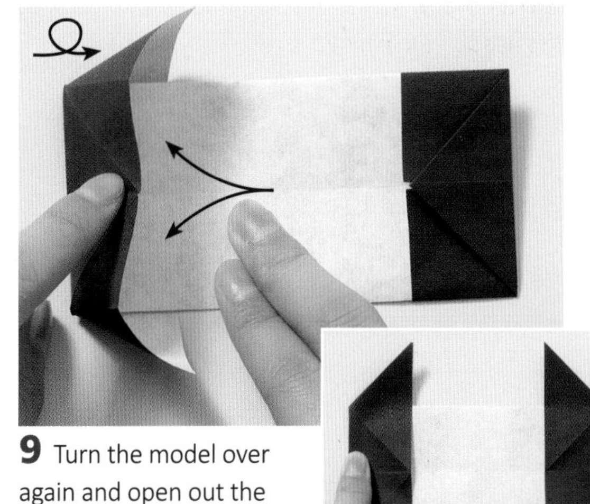

9 Turn the model over again and open out the left-hand flap, refolding it so that the creases reverse and triangles are formed above and below the model. Repeat on the right-hand side.

Addict! 99% of a panda's diet consists of bamboo shoots.

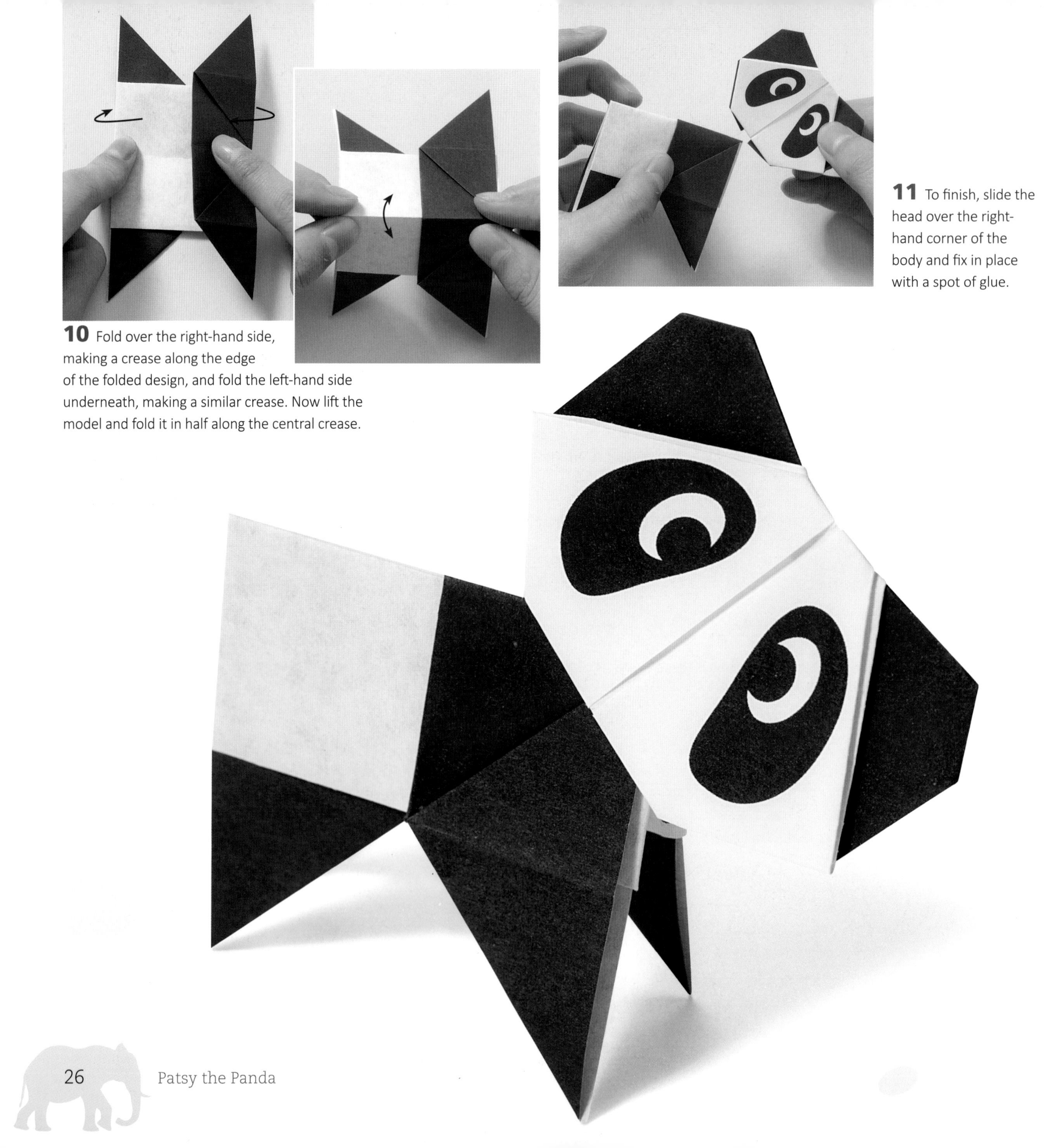

10 Fold over the right-hand side, making a crease along the edge of the folded design, and fold the left-hand side underneath, making a similar crease. Now lift the model and fold it in half along the central crease.

11 To finish, slide the head over the right-hand corner of the body and fix in place with a spot of glue.

Ezra the Elephant

Elephants are one of the few animals known to express emotions, and here we've made one with a happy expression simply by cutting into the sides of the face with a pair of scissors. This also gives Ellie her long trunk. Did you know that an elephant's trunk contains an incredible 40,000 muscles? The elephant uses it to lift food and suck up water.

1 With the 10in (25cm) sheet of paper face down, make a crease from corner to corner between the eyes on the design, then open out.

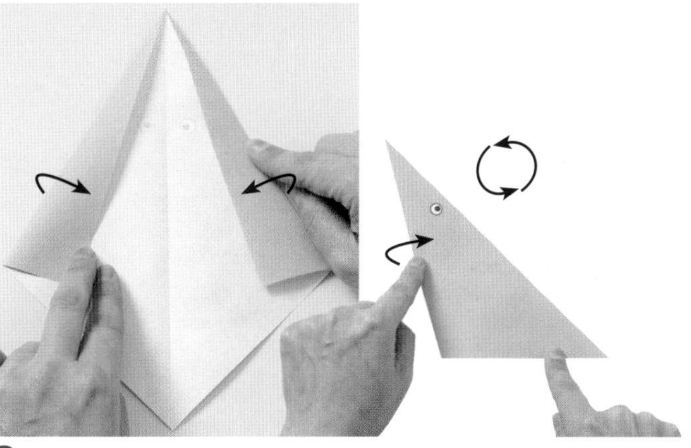

2 Fold in the upper sides, making creases between the top corner and a point approximately 2in (5cm) above the side corner, making sure that both sides are identical. Fold the paper in half and twist it so that the shortest side is nearest you.

3 Fold the top half of the model to the right, making a crease between the bottom left corner and a point about halfway along the longest edge, ensuring that the new top edge is close to horizontal.

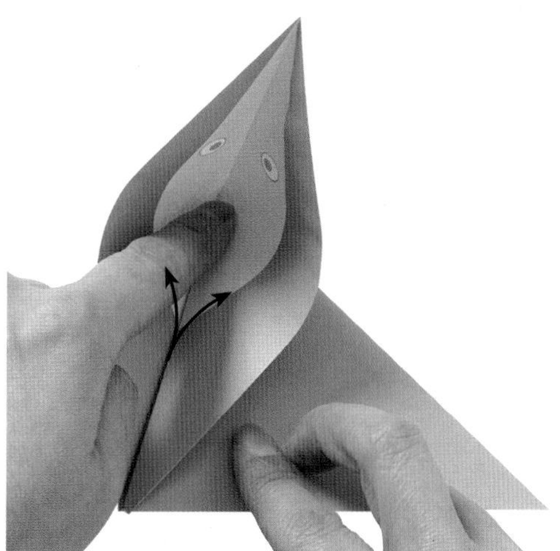

4 Lift the top flap and open it out, folding the point forward so that it is in line with the corner of the model underneath.

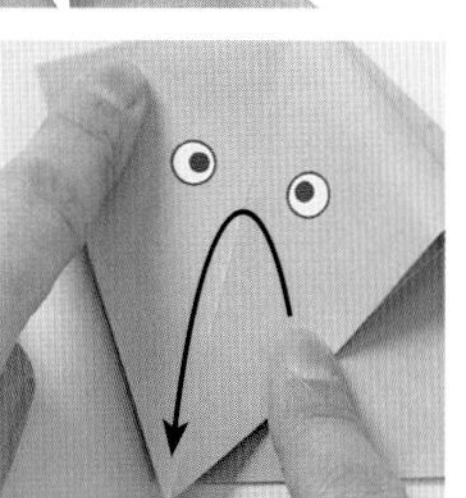

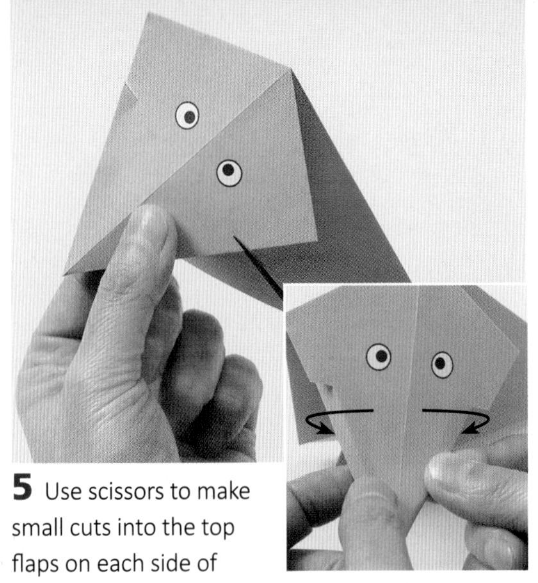

5 Use scissors to make small cuts into the top flaps on each side of the face just below the eyes, ensuring they are exactly opposite each other. Fold in the edges of the face from the end of each cut to the bottom point.

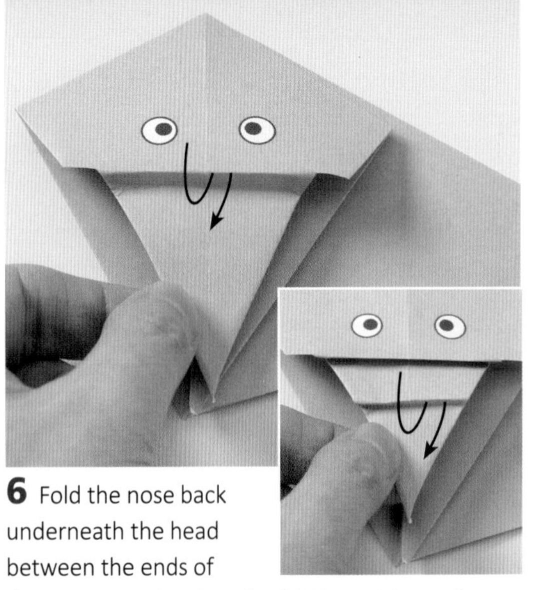

6 Fold the nose back underneath the head between the ends of the cuts, ensuring that the fold is at right angles to the central crease, and then fold the nose back ¼in (5mm) further down. Repeat the double fold 1in (2.5cm) nearer the tip of the nose.

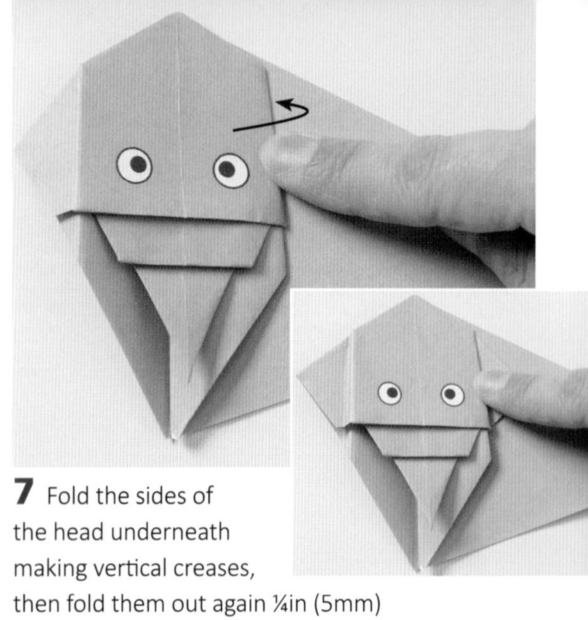

7 Fold the sides of the head underneath making vertical creases, then fold them out again ¼in (5mm) further out to make the ears.

8 Fold back the tail 3in (8cm) from the corner of the model, then fold back the tip so that it ends up well beyond the crease you made first.

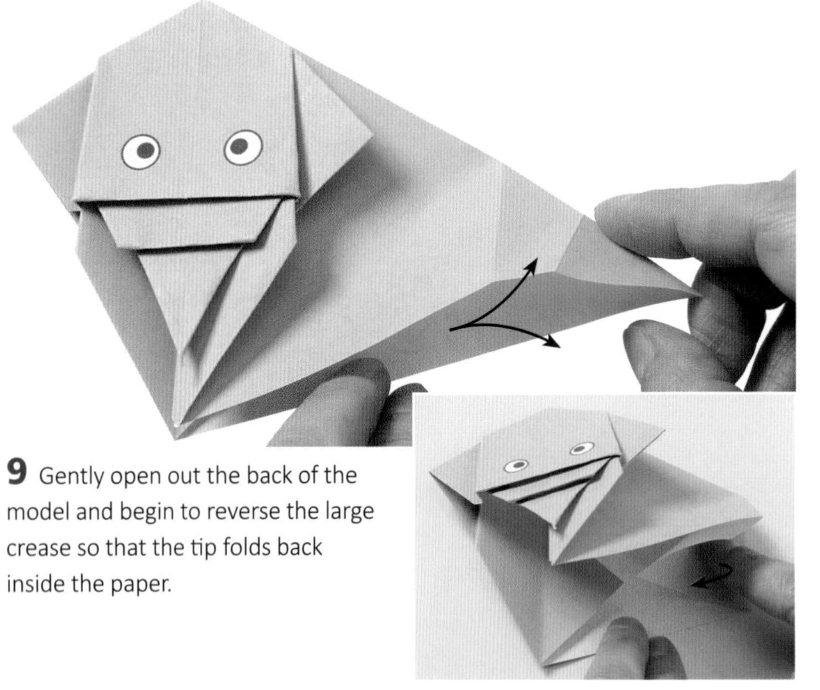

9 Gently open out the back of the model and begin to reverse the large crease so that the tip folds back inside the paper.

Splash! When elephants swim, their trunk acts as a snorkel so they can breathe!

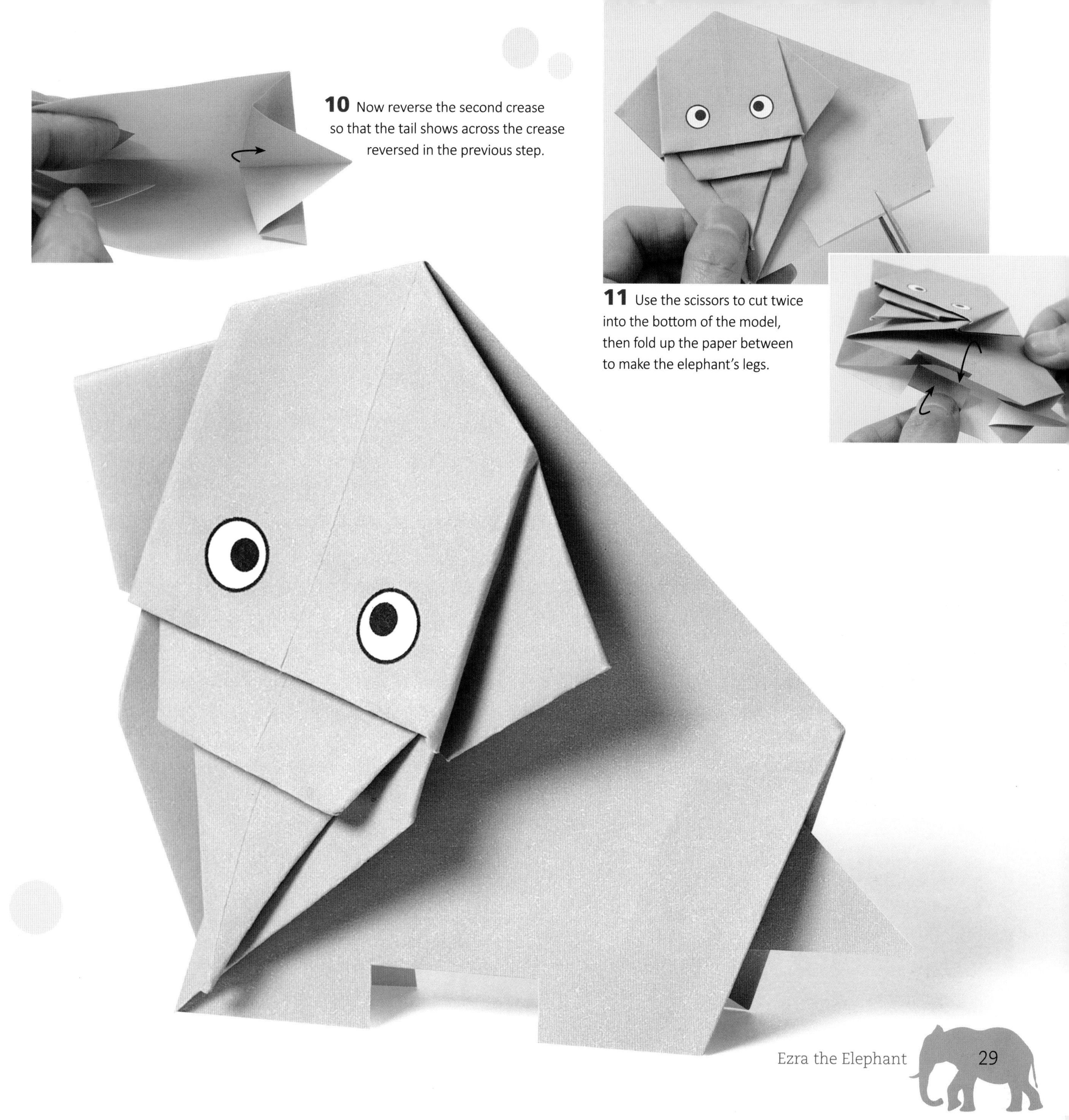

10 Now reverse the second crease so that the tail shows across the crease reversed in the previous step.

11 Use the scissors to cut twice into the bottom of the model, then fold up the paper between to make the elephant's legs.

Pippa the Penguin

The penguin has two distinct colors, as seen on this model. Its black back camouflages it when viewed from above in the ocean; its white underside camouflages it when viewed from below the water against the bright surface. How clever! Penguins tend to keep the same mate, so use your second piece of penguin paper to make a friend for Pippa!

1 With the 10in (25cm) sheet of paper face down and the eyes closest to you, fold the sheet in half to make a crease from corner to corner through the middle of the design, then open it out again.

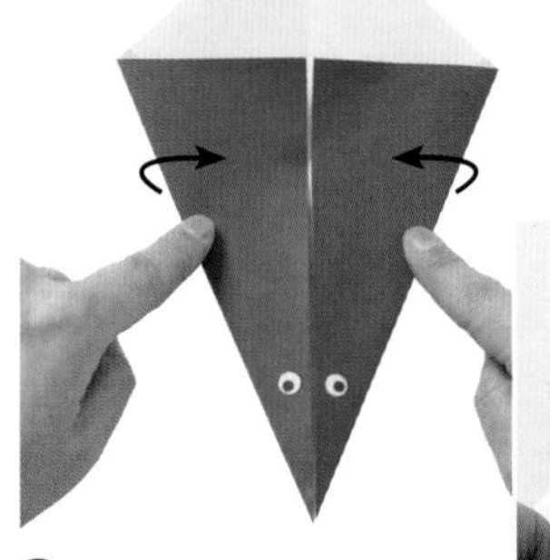

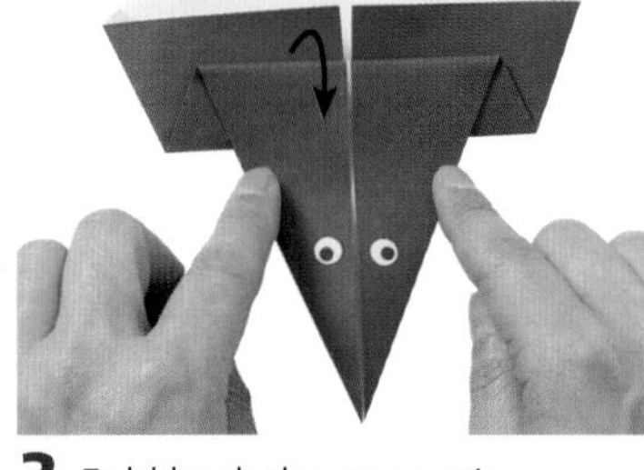

2 Fold the two side points in so that the edges meet along the central crease, then fold the bottom tip up so that it sits on top of the top tip.

3 Fold back the upper tip, making a second crease halfway across the colored part of the paper showing, then turn the nose underneath just below the eyes. Turn it back again, making another crease 1in (2.5cm) closer to the tip.

4 Fold the model in half right along the central crease.

5 Turn back the bottom left tip of the main part of the model, making a crease from the left-hand tip to a point ¾in (2cm) from the right-hand edge. Turn the model over and repeat before turning it back again.

6 Turn the bottom of the model over to the right, using the diagonal edge as a guide for the crease line.

7 Pick up the model and open it out slightly, turning the head downward. Close up the model again, reversing the creases, and make an outside fold to form the penguin's head.

8 Fold over the bottom left-hand corner to make a vertical crease, then turn the tip back again so that it just crosses the fold just made.

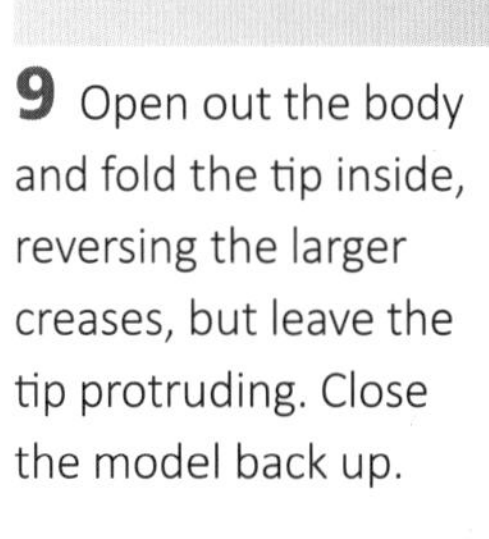

9 Open out the body and fold the tip inside, reversing the larger creases, but leave the tip protruding. Close the model back up.

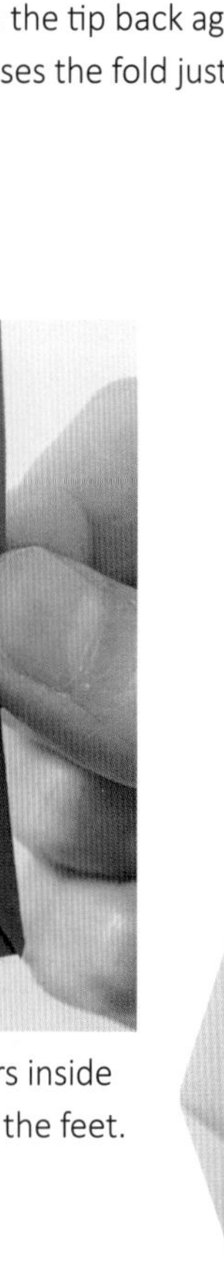

10 Fold the bottom corners inside at an angle to show more of the feet.

I wish I could fly! Penguins are flightless birds, with flippers instead of wings.

About the authors

Mari Ono is an expert in origami and all forms of papercrafts. Born in Japan, she has lived in the UK for many years with her artist husband, Takumasa, where they both work to promote Japanese arts and crafts. Her other books include the best-selling *The Simple Art of Origami, Origami for Children, More Origami for Children, How to Make Paper Planes and Other Flying Objects, Wild and Wonderful Origami, Origami for Mindfulness,* and *Origami Farm*, all available from CICO Books.

Fumiaki Shingu was born in Japan. He is the creator of "JOYD" products and the founder of Origami Club (www.origami-club.com), which was created in 2002.

Suppliers

Origami paper is available at most good paper stores or online. Try searching online for "origami paper" to find a whole range of stores, selling a wide variety of paper, that will send packages directly to your home.

UK

HOBBYCRAFT
www.hobbycraft.co.uk
TEL: +44 (0)330 026 1400

JP-BOOKS
www.jpbooks.co.uk
TEL: +44 (0)20 7839 4839
info@jpbooks.co.uk

JAPAN CENTRE
www.japancentre.com
TEL: +44 (0)20 3405 1151
enquiry@japancentre.com

THE JAPANESE SHOP
www.thejapaneseshop.co.uk
TEL: +44 (0) 1423 876320
info@thejapaneseshop.co.uk

USA

A.C. MOORE
www.acmoore.com
Stores nationwide
TEL: 1-888-226-6673

HOBBY LOBBY
www.hobbylobby.com
Stores nationwide
TEL: 1-800-888-0321

JO-ANN FABRIC AND CRAFT STORE
www.joann.com
Stores nationwide
TEL: 1-888-739-4120

MICHAELS STORES
www.michaels.com
Stores nationwide
TEL: 1-800-642-4235

HAKUBUNDO (HONOLULU, HAWAII)
www.hakubundo.com
TEL: (808) 947-5503
web@hakubundo.com

Thanks to Minako Ishibashi for the Panda design and Taiko Niwa for the Gorilla design.

18 sheets of origami paper

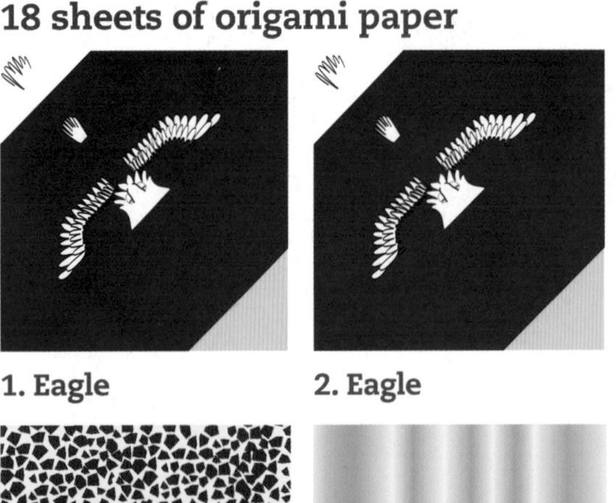

1. Eagle

2. Eagle

3. Snake

4. Giraffe

5. Giraffe

6. Chameleon

7. Zebra

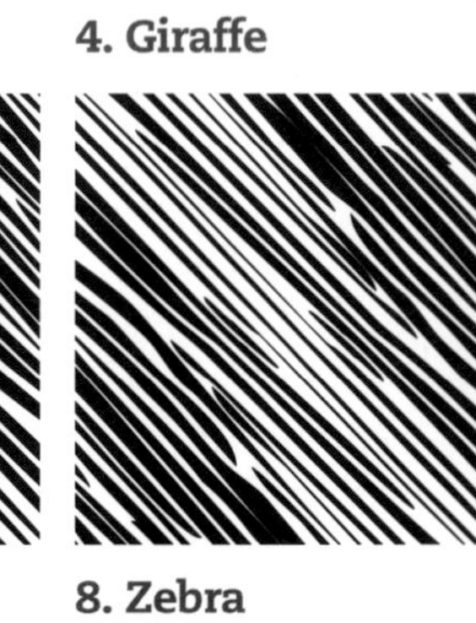

8. Zebra

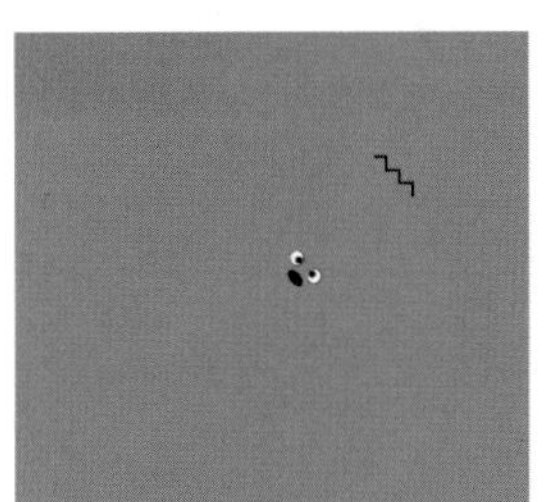

9. Monkey

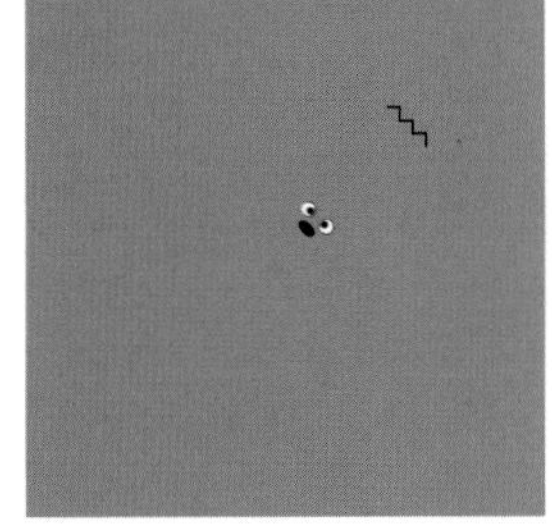

10. Monkey

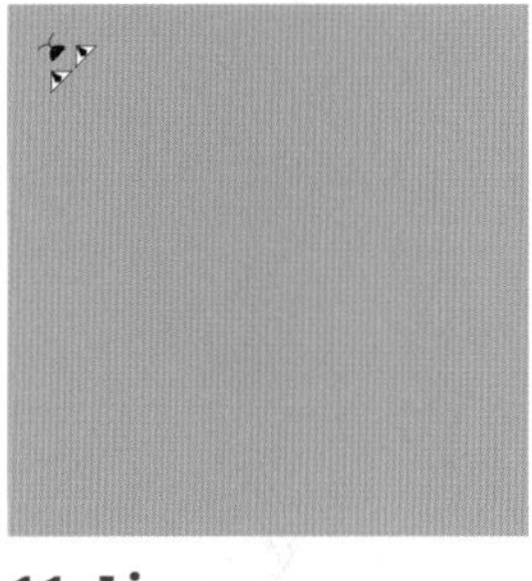

11. Lion

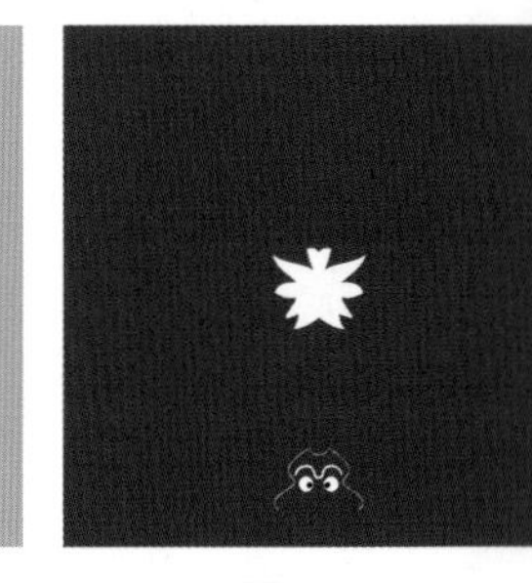

12. Gorilla

13. Cheetah

14. Panda

15. Panda

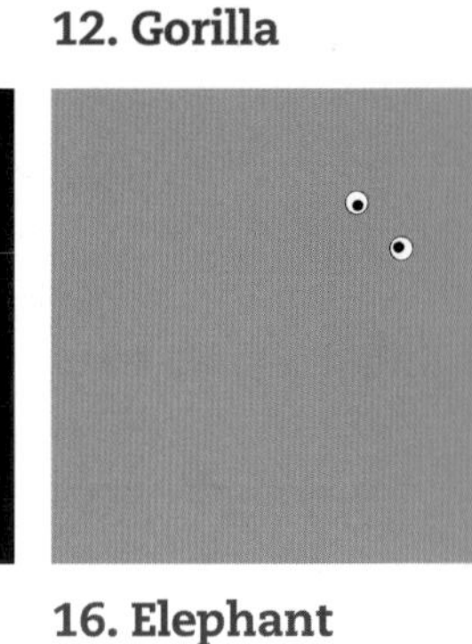

16. Elephant

17. Penguin

18. Penguin

You only need one sheet of paper for each project, but we have given you additional papers to make two eagles, giraffes, zebras, monkeys, pandas, and penguins. Your animals can go two by two!

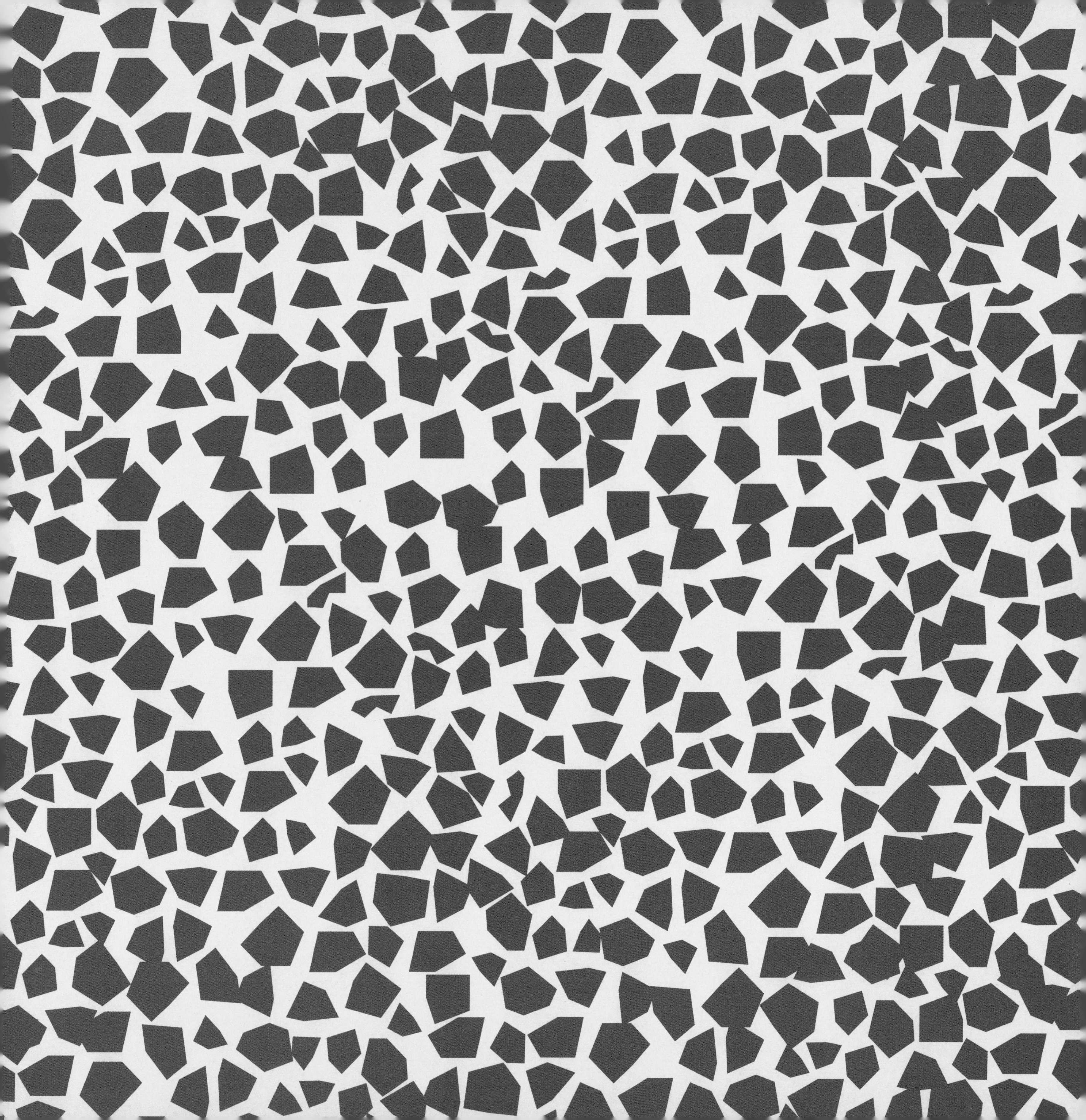

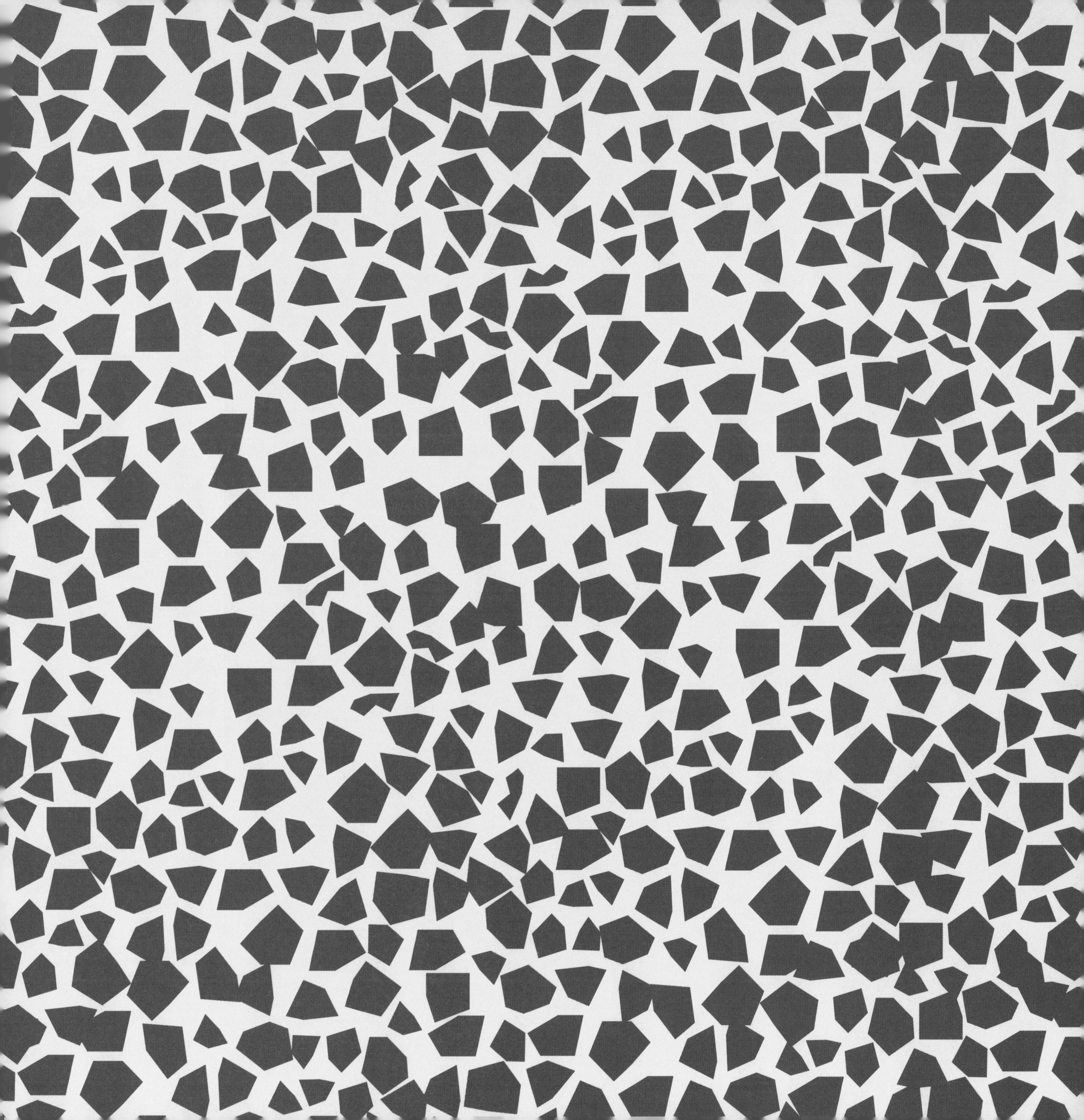

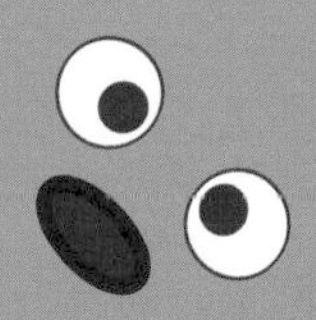